Dedicated to those who seek the truth.

CONTENTS

MISSION finder

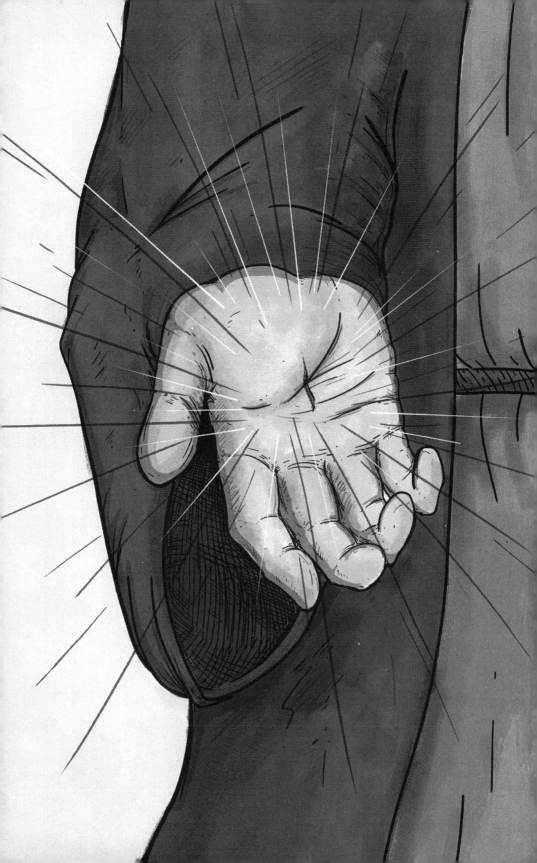

THIRTY DAY COMMITMENT

God, I hereby express a sincere desire to better understand *your* will for my life.

I am ready to learn how to find my mission here on earth. Let the thirty-day journey begin …

Reader's Signature:

_____

Accountability Partner #1 Signature:

_____

Accountability Partner #2 Signature:

_____

Location & Date:

_____

Therefore do not be foolish, but understand what the Lord's will is.
—Ephesians 5:17 (NIV)

YOUR PATH TO PROGRESS

Life is a series of choices and decisions that will determine the positive and negative results in your life. At the end of each chapter, you will be presented with a *Path to Progress* page. Use this section to apply the information you learn in this book. Avoid the temptation to brush over these pages or rush through this part of the daily devotional. This is where the revelation takes place.

The *Path to Progress* section is an essential study tool to see transformation in your life. It's a time for you to reflect, pray, meditate, and consider your choices and decisions in life. It's an opportunity for you to express your innermost desires to God and study His promises. Each day, you will examine one question that Jesus asked those around Him while He was here on earth and four questions to ask yourself. Lastly, you will be challenged to make a commitment to move forward with a daily call to action.

Pace yourself. *Mission Finder* is a thirty-day journey to reveal your heart. This book will help you gain insight, knowledge, and understanding to find God's will for your life and point you in the right direction toward fulfilling His will.

Spend time with God. Open your Bible. While meditating on each *Path to Progress*, read around each verse referenced. Remember, it is through intimacy and prayer that the Holy Spirit can access your heart. This is where eternal transformation begins.

I have no greater joy than to hear that my children are walking in the truth.
—3 John 1:4 (NIV)

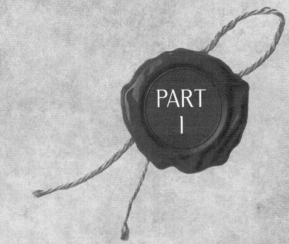

PART
I

FIND GOD'S WILL FOR YOUR LIFE

INTRODUCTION

You were born to fulfill God's will. When you seek God's will for your life, you will discover your mission. Every one of us is being prepared to carry out God's will. The question is … *Will you accept your mission?* For most of us, there are major obstacles that hold us back from fulfilling our missions. Common obstacles include doubt and unbelief or disobedience and apathy. God has given us clear, concise instructions on what our mission is here on earth. *So what's the problem?* The cares of this world are the roadblocks to fulfilling God's will.

Embrace Spiritual Growth

In the business world, entrepreneurs are taught to create companies that will solve industry-specific problems. *"What problem are you solving?"* is an everyday question between a venture capitalist and an entrepreneur. Just like entrepreneurs need to identify problems in their industries to solve, believers in Christ need to take a similar approach when identifying problems in their spiritual growth. God has given us the tools, wisdom, and knowledge through His living word to overcome any obstacle, roadblock, or personal problem we may be facing.

The problems in our personal and spiritual lives go unresolved because we seek an external solution to solve an internal issue. To relieve pain, we take a pill. To discover purpose, we follow others who have found their purposes. To fill the holes in our hearts, we accumulate, consume, or even develop new relationships to make us feel better. Our selfish desires do not sleep. Even in our dreams, we wrestle with ourselves. The human heart has an endless appetite that seeks out its own purpose.

Identify Your True Identity

Your identity plays the leading role in the movie of your life. **Who you are is a child of God.** The sooner you accept the "child" part of that statement, the sooner you can walk in His will. As an obedient child follows the footsteps of his mother and father, an obedient child of God carries out the will of his Father. The child grows up to fulfill the Father's will and learns how to bear much fruit for his Father's kingdom.

You are magnificent in God's eyes. As a child of God, you have a destiny. You were not a mistake. God does not make mistakes. You are exactly who you were designed to be. You are you. When you come to the revelation that you are custom-made, unique, and beautiful, you realize that you were perfectly designed for such a moment as this in world history. You are adored from the heavens above, and you are loved despite your shortcomings.

Identify Your True Purpose

The universal questions of life are: Who am I? What am I doing here? Where did I come from? When did this all begin, and when does it all end? Why am I alive? How did I get here? What do I do with my life? These foundational questions resonate in the hearts, minds, and souls of every human being on earth. Only one book in human history has been able to address and answer every one of those questions with absolute truth. Without mentioning this book's name, its subject matter, or its author(s), you already know the book I am talking about. It's the best seller of all time, the inerrant word of God—the Bible.

Deep within your heart, you know there is good and evil, right and wrong. You know this world is not a cosmic accident. You know there is evidence of intelligent design surrounding you. Recognition of these truths is the beginning of wisdom, knowledge, and the answers to your universal questions.

Identify Your True Mission

What does God want you to do with your life? In order to answer that question, you need to discover what God's *will* is and what God's *plan* is for your life. Then you can align your will with His will and your desires with His desires.

Mission Finder is a thirty-day journey. Part One is the first twelve days of your journey for you to learn how to *find* God's will for your life. In Part One, you will focus on three discovery steps to help you get started.

- Step 1 is to *define your mission*. What is God's will for your life?
- Step 2 is to *clarify your vision*. What does God see in you?
- Step 3 is to *follow your leader*. What does God want you to do?

Part Two is the next eighteen days of your journey for you to learn how to fulfill God's will for your life. Do you know what God's will is for your life? Are you clear on your mission? Only you can answer these questions. Why doesn't God just tell you? Because discovering God's will builds hope, faith, and trust in Him. It also helps you discern His voice. In order to truly understand His will for your life, you need to turn introspective and take a look at your own will.

Let's get underway on an exciting journey as you discover God's will for your life and you move toward hearing those precious words we all long for … "Well done, good and faithful servant."

step one

DEFINE YOUR MISSION

WHAT IS GOD'S WILL FOR YOUR LIFE?

YOUR WILL

"The gateway to life is very narrow and the road is difficult, and only a few ever find it." [1]

Your will is what determines your path in life. It's what guides you. It's what gets you up in the morning. Waking up every morning knowing that you are doing exactly what you were designed to do, which is to carry out God's will for your life, is an amazing feeling that doesn't get old. The best part of waking up should not be the coffee in your cup. The best part of waking up should be knowing the day ahead is full of adventure, life-changing moments, and divine appointments.

As a *good person* walking Planet Earth, you may define *your will* to be something like this:

My will is to live well. My will is to fulfill the desires of my heart. My will is to succeed in life. My will is to learn more about God. My will is to increase my knowledge about the Bible. My will is to attend and tithe to my local church. My will is to help others once I have taken care of myself and my needs. My will is to spend time with and take care of my loved ones. My will is to surround myself with others who share my morals, ethics, and values. My will is to be accepted by others. My will is not to hurt anyone's feelings. My will is to share the gospel when appropriate and to do my best to make sure not to offend anyone. My will is to do my best to reflect righteousness in public. My will is to try to figure out what to do with the rest of my life to serve God. My will is not to waste my life. My will is *my will*, but I'm not exactly sure what *God's will* is for my life.

Be honest. Did any of those examples resonate with you? If so, you are primed and ready to discover God's will for your life. **Here is the good, the bad, and the ugly.** The good news is that you are on the right path and will have all the information you need in this book to find God's will for your life. The bad news is that unless you apply this information, you will never see any transformation to fulfill God's will. The ugly is that if you proclaim to be a Bible-believing Christian *saved by grace* and the blood of your Savior, Jesus Christ, and choose not to obey God's will, you risk the incomprehensible. Jesus was clear when He said:

*"Not everyone who calls out to me, 'Lord! Lord!' will enter the Kingdom of Heaven. **Only those who actually do the will of my Father in heaven will enter.** On judgment day many will say to me, 'Lord! Lord! We prophesied in your name and cast out demons in your name and performed many miracles in your name.' But I will reply, 'I never knew you. Get away from me, **you who break God's laws.'"** [2]*

At first glance, you may be thinking, "Wait a minute, I thought we were all *saved by grace?"* The modern-day church predominantly teaches the gospel of grace. The cornerstone verse we have been taught in the "saved by grace" movement is: *For it is by grace you have been saved, through faith—and this is not from yourselves, it is the gift of God—not by works, so that no one can boast.* [3]

The truth is we *are* saved by grace—**through faith.** The key phrase in this verse is *through faith,* yet the modern-day focus is on *by grace.* What exactly did the author mean by *through faith?* Faith is commonly defined as hope of the unseen. Faith requires belief. Belief requires acceptance of a truth, and our actions are a result of what we believe. In order to believe in something, you must first agree with it. You cannot truly believe in something while simultaneously ignoring the agreement that created that belief in the first place. Although you cannot earn your salvation, you can choose whether to agree with your leader's commands and, most importantly, whether to obey them. When you choose to place your faith in Jesus, your obedience is the essential element to validate your agreement of faith in Him.

Jesus didn't say His grace has saved you. He said *your faith* has saved you. *"Your faith has saved you. Go in peace."* [4]

If you are saved by grace *through faith*, not your works, as Paul tells us, why does *doing God's will* even matter? And if you choose not to do His will (i.e. break His laws), how can you be *saved by grace* yet be rejected from entering heaven? It doesn't make sense. This presents a significant conflict to the modern-day believer.

Without doubt, most Christians can agree the Word of God is inerrant, so how can these two verses coexist? From a scholar's perspective, one might argue that Jesus's promises (words) would take seniority over Paul's promises (words). To spare you the theological debate, let me share what is revealed inside that Scripture for all to see. Jesus left us with two nuggets of wisdom to solve this equation within the verse when He said:

"Only those who actually do the will of my Father in heaven will enter." [5]
"Get away from me, you who break God's laws." [6]

Jesus didn't say, "Only those of you who believe in me and my Father, *through grace*, will enter." He specifically said: "Only those who actually **do the will of my Father** in heaven will enter." That is one hundred percent clear. Then Jesus said, "Get away from me, you who break God's laws." Again, one hundred percent clear.

The two main points Jesus highlighted were:
1. You *must* do the will of His Father to enter the kingdom of heaven.
2. You *cannot* claim to "know Him" and continuously break God's laws at the same time.

Christ addressed the importance of obeying God's laws in His teachings throughout the Gospels when He said:
"Anyone who listens to my teaching and follows it is wise." [7]
"Anyone who hears my teaching and doesn't obey it is foolish." [8]

"Anyone who loves me will obey my teaching." [9]

Jesus spoke the truth at all times to believers and nonbelievers alike. He was clear when discussing God's laws when He said: *"Until heaven and earth disappear, not even the smallest detail of God's law will disappear until its purpose is achieved."* [10]

So what does all of this mean? It means you can't truly believe God is who He says He is, accept Him, and have faith in Him, and then break, ignore, or disobey His laws and commands. By breaking, ignoring, or flat-out disobeying His commands, your unbelief in His divinity reveals itself. It also means, if you take Jesus at His word, you must do the will of the Father to enter the kingdom of heaven.

Keep my commands and you will live;
guard my teachings as the apple of your eye. [11]

When you choose to obey God's commands, you are signing up for eternity. When you meet someone who's living the life God designed them to live, you know it. It's exciting and inspiring to be around them. Their joy, aspiration, motivation, and encouragement are something to behold. This is the life that God desires for you to live. If you ignore God's will, your life will turn out much differently. Throughout the book, we will uncover what God promises you when you follow Him, including protection, joy, and His presence.

For the LORD loves justice,
And does not forsake His saints;
They are preserved forever,
But the descendants of the wicked shall be cut off. [12]

The greatest risk in life is pursuing your own will. Without consideration for God's will, you have no protection or guarantee of the end result. The odds are against you from day one. If you believe that God loves justice ... if you believe God will never abandon the godly ... if you believe God will keep His saints safe forever, you actually have no risk whatsoever as you find and fulfill God's will. The risk is in pursuing your own will. By pursuing your will, you create a tremendous amount of risk for yourself. You have no promise, no protection, and no security that you will be safe from the result of your choices and decisions. By pursuing your will, following your self-interest, you are counting on your wisdom and your results.

Great are your purposes and mighty are your deeds. Your eyes are open to the ways of all mankind; you reward each person according to their conduct and as their deeds deserve. [13]

When you choose the right path, your life becomes worth living. If you have selected the wrong path, you may frequently question your existence. You have the ability to change your path with a simple choice. Choose a path leading to a lifestyle that is righteous, just, and fair.

"I desire to do your will, my God; your law is within my heart." [14]

God wants you to enjoy carrying out His will. Just like a father takes joy in watching his children do something well that he has taught them, God takes joy in watching you abound in your life. Learn to love finding God's will. Learn to love doing God's will. Learn to love fulfilling God's will. It will become your greatest joy in life. Waking up each morning knowing that you have a purpose, there is a plan, and you have been assigned a specific mission that God has designed just for you to accomplish is a magnificent feeling. *But you are a chosen generation, a royal priesthood, a holy nation, His own special people, that you may proclaim the praises of Him who called you out of darkness into His marvelous light.* [15]

When pursuing God's will, you will quickly come to the realization that God is working through you, but you will also realize that He designed you with special talents and gifts to carry out His will exactly at this point in time in human history. Let that thought sink in for a moment.

The truth is God promises each and every one of us in His Word that every single one of us is capable and was specifically designed to carry out His missions. *For we are His workmanship, created in Christ Jesus for good works, which God prepared beforehand that we should walk in them.* [16]

Are you ready to find your mission? Start today by expressing a sincere desire to seek His will.

Mission Principle 1
Sincere faith in God is expressed by doing His will.

Path to Progress

Desire to find joy in doing God's will. *Psalm 40:8*
Choose to obey God's laws so you can live. *Proverbs 7:2*
Decide to act with righteousness, justice, and fairness. *Proverbs 1:3*
The **result** is a great reward will await you if you obey God's laws.
Psalm 19:11
The **promise** is God loves justice. He will never abandon you if you're
godly. He will protect you forever. *Psalm 37:28*

Question from Jesus
"Why do you call me, 'Lord, Lord,' and do not do what I say?" [17]

Questions to Meditate On
What exactly is God's will?
Am I obeying the teachings of Jesus?
Do I know God's will for *my* life?
Am I seeking God's will?

Your Call to Action
Learn God's will. Obey God's commands.
Read them. Meditate on them. Follow them.

JESUS'S WILL

"For my Father's will is that everyone who looks to the Son and believes in him shall have eternal life, and I will raise them up at the last day." [1]

A true disciple of Jesus is on a mission to become Christ-like. Jesus clearly spelled out God's will for His life and all believers' lives within the Scripture. Let's slip on the shoes of Christ for a moment to see what His will was while here on earth and how that contrasts with today's traditional cultural Christian. Jesus's signature statement about His will during His time on earth was:

"The Spirit of the Lord is on me,
because he has anointed me
to proclaim good news to the poor.
He has sent me to proclaim freedom for the prisoners
and recovery of sight for the blind,
to set the oppressed free." [2]

In His words throughout the Gospels, Jesus further proclaimed:
- My will is my Father's will. [3]
- My will is to love my Father. [4]
- My will is to be obedient to my Father. [5]
- My will is to abide in my Father's love. [6]
- My will is to follow the commandments of my Father. [7]
- My will is to do what the Father does. [8]
- My will is to fulfill the will of my Father's heart. [9]
- My will is to be one with my Father in a moment to moment relationship. [10]
- My will is to reflect the Father's righteous ways. [11]

+ My will is to lay down and sacrifice my life for others. [12]
+ My will is to heal those who are sick and brokenhearted. [13]
+ My will is to lead others to eternal life through salvation. [14]
+ My will is to speak the truth regardless of offense or consequences. [15]
+ My will is to seek the kingdom of God above all else in my life. [16]
+ My will is to increase the kingdom of God. [17]

Jesus was focused on God's will. Jesus desired for His Father to lead Him. He didn't try to do things on His own. Instead, He followed. Jesus respected His Father. He revered His Father with a healthy fear. If Jesus were to summarize His will in a love letter, I believe it would read:

Father,
Moment by moment, I sense your love and protection over me. I desire nothing in this world but to please you. I am here for you, ready to do anything you command. Whatever your heart desires is my command. I will carry it out for you. It brings me great joy to share your truth with others. It brings me greater joy to seek your kingdom above all else. I am honored you have sent me to heal the sick, to set those who are afflicted free, and to bring salvation to those who believe in you through me. At your command, I am ready to sacrifice my life for others.
Your son,
Jesus

The LORD is my shepherd, I lack nothing. [18]

The fear of the LORD is the beginning of knowledge,
But fools despise wisdom and instruction. [19]

To fear the Lord is to revere the Lord. When you revere the Lord and everything He stands for, you set yourself up for spiritual growth. When you do not respect the Lord, you ignore His commandments, or you disobey Him, you set yourself up for failure. If you fail to acknowledge

Jesus, you are actually shouting and raising your fist at God as if you are against Him. If you don't acknowledge Jesus, you certainly can't revere God.

Think about someone in your life who does not respect you. Do you have any motivation or incentive to go out of your way to try to bless that person? Usually not. Why is that? Because that person has insulted you, not properly valued you, and many times has broken your trust. If it's a long-standing relationship or a family member, you may still love that person but you realize that you cannot support that person given their disrespect.

Now imagine this same scenario between you and a child. If your child does not respect, revere, or obey you, that doesn't mean you don't love your child. However, like any loving parent, you desire for your child to be obedient. In the meantime, you will not be supporting your child's behavior. Why? Because you love your child and you know better. You don't want to create a false reality for the child. You want to teach them the right way.

"Truly I tell you, unless you change and become like little children, you will never enter the kingdom of heaven." [20]

Finally, put this scenario into context between God and His children. By giving God the proper respect and reverence that He deserves, you set yourself up for clear communication. Your obedience to Him through respect and reverence is the essential ingredient for your spiritual growth. **This is what it means to fear the Lord.**

My eyes are ever on the LORD,
for only He will release my feet from the snare. [21]

When you draw near to Jesus, He will draw near to you. These days, there are so many things demanding your attention and attracting your eyes. Keeping a laser focus on Jesus is the solution to avoid distraction.

By keeping your eyes on Him, you are inviting Him into your life. By calling out to Jesus, you are letting Him know that you need Him, that you can't do it by yourself. When you reach for Jesus, He will be there. You can start with this prayer today.

> Lord Jesus, I need you. My eyes are now focused on you, not on the things of this world. Please take my distractions away from me and replace them with things that you desire. Let me see through your eyes. Let me see what you see. Let me hear what you hear. Let me feel what you feel. I want to be like you. I don't have it all figured out. I'm trusting that you will teach me your ways, that you will show me the right path, that you will guide me the right way and stay with me every step of the journey. I become afraid, I become doubtful, but through your Holy Spirit, I overcome those doubts and fears. Help me find God's will. Teach me how to be obedient. Show me how to fulfill God's will just like you did.

The LORD confides in those who fear him;
He makes his covenant known to them. [22]

Respect the Lord. Revere Him as the king that He is. The fear of the Lord is different from the fear of man or fear of the unknown. The fear of the Lord is a healthy type of fear. Fear of man or fear of the unknown is paralyzing and disabling. These kinds of fears are unhealthy types of fear. When you fear the Lord, He knows that you will use His covenants for good. By cherishing Him, you show Him reverence, and in turn, He shows you love and mercy.

The fear of the LORD is the beginning of wisdom,
and knowledge of the Holy One is understanding. [23]

Fear and wisdom lead to understanding. What does fearing the Lord have to do with the beginning of wisdom? Why would fear result in wisdom? And why would you need to fear God in order to start understanding wisdom? The reason that the fear of the Lord is the beginning of wisdom is because without recognition of God's authority, anything that you deem wisdom could be attributed to your own intelligence. Without recognizing that all things come from God and all wisdom is imparted by God, there would be no reason to fear God. This fear of the Lord is what Jesus exercised here on earth. This is how He was able to find and fulfill God's will. By following Jesus's example, you can do the same.

After clearly understanding Jesus's will, which is to do the will of His Father, and understanding how to fear the Lord, the next step is for you to understand God's will.

Mission Principle 2
Your destiny is to become Christ-like.

Path to Progress

Desire the Lord as your shepherd. *Psalm 23:1*
Choose to keep your eyes always on God. *Psalm 25:15*
Decide to fear the Lord. *Proverbs 1:7*
The **result** is He teaches His covenant to you if you fear him.
Psalm 25:14
The **promise** is God's goodness and faithful love will follow you all the
days of your life. *Psalm 23:6*

Question from Jesus
"Shall I not drink the cup the Father has given me?" [24]

Questions to Meditate On
How can you apply Jesus's will in your own life?
Does your character reflect Christ to others?
What characteristics of Christ do you feel you lack?
Do you have a desire to change your character?

Your Call to Action
Study Jesus. Model His methods.
Develop His attributes. Understand Jesus's will.

GOD'S WILL

Trust in the LORD with all your heart;
do not depend on your own understanding.
Seek his will in all you do,
and he will show you which path to take. [1]

All wisdom comes from above. God is the granter of such wisdom. Pay attention to Him. If you desire to seek Him, seek God's will as priority one in your life. When you seek God's will in all that you do, He will show you the right path.

Come and listen to my counsel.
I'll share my heart with you
and make you wise. [2]

If God were to summarize His will for your life in a love letter, I believe it would read:

My precious son/daughter,
Be strong and courageous, not fearful. [3] I'm here to strengthen you and uphold you with righteousness. [4] Acknowledge me; trust me with all of your heart. Do not lean on your own understanding. [5] Do not get caught up in worldly possessions or the desires of your eyes. [6] Be thankful and grateful in all circumstances. [7] Avoid sexual immorality. [8] Be sanctified by my Holy Spirit. [9] Silence the talk of foolish people by your righteous behavior. [10] Renew your mind and do not be conformed to the ways of this world. [11] Rather, live by the fruit of the Spirit. [12]

I have a purpose for you. Be called to that purpose by loving me. [13] Follow my will; [14] I will provide you a hope and a future. [15] I will give to you generously and provide you wisdom. [16] I just ask that you love me above all else. [17] I long to give you the desires of your heart. [18] I will forgive you for all of your sins, cleanse you from all unrighteousness, [19] and help you overcome temptation. [20] Accept my Son, Jesus, so that you may inherit eternal life and not perish. [21] Follow His commands and make disciples. [22] Love His followers like family. [23] Follow His example so that you will bear much fruit in your life [24] and bring the kingdom of heaven to earth. [25] Receive the reward I have promised you. [26] Seek the kingdom first and everything will be added to you. [27] I will equip you with everything you need to carry out your mission. [28] Seek my presence continually. Rely on me; do all things through me for I will strengthen you. [29] Do not worry; I will provide every need of yours. [30]
Your loving Father, now and forever,
Dad

Throughout the Bible, God shares His will for your life.
+ God's will is that you seek His will in all that you do. [31]
+ God's will is that you find Him by praying to Him with all of your heart. [32]
+ God's will is for you to continue to do good in the midst of suffering. [33]
+ God's will is for you to find out if Jesus's teachings come from God. [34]
+ God's will is for you to do what is right, to love mercy, and walk humbly with Him. [35]
+ God's will is that you do all things through Him who strengthens you. [36]
+ God's will is that you reject the acts of the flesh. [37]
+ God's will is that no one should perish. [38]
+ God's will is that Jesus should lose none of the people who He gave to Jesus. [39]

See Appendix 1 for more verses about God's will for your life.

God already knows the desires of your heart. He knows the things that you want, but as long as you pursue them on your own time, of your own accord, with your own terms and conditions, you will continue to get *your own* results. What I've found is the more that I submit and surrender to *His* will, the more He opens up and blesses the desires in my heart. The more I grow closer to Him, the more my desires align with His.

It all starts with the *decision* to seek *His will* in all that you do. After you make this decision, there will be a hunger to seek God's knowledge. You will learn to depend on the Holy Spirit to show you how to apply this information in your life. You will start to live fully dependent on the Holy Spirit, seeking His counsel on how to find and fulfill God's will. Your focus and priority will be doing God's work. He will show you the way. He will give you the things that you need. He will provide for you in the capacity that He sees fit. He designed you, so of course He knows what you need. He created you especially for a season and a time such as this.

Finding God's will isn't about changing who you are. God made you who you are, the way you are. Finding God's will is about changing your heart's priorities and making His passions a priority over your own passions. Put Him first, so that He may show you how much He loves you.

This leads us to the next part of your journey, which is to better understand how to apply God's will in your life through Father God's business.

Mission Principle 3
Make God's will the primary desire of your heart.

Day 3

Path to Progress

Desire to seek His will in all you do. *Proverbs 3:5*
Choose to put your hope in God all day long. *Psalm 25:5*
Decide to be strong and have courage. *Psalm 31:24*
The **result** is God will share His heart with you and help you become
wise. And that you will find peace, and fear and harm won't trouble you.
Proverbs 1:23, 33
The **promise** is God will be a friend to you if you fear Him. *Psalm 25:14*

Question from Jesus
"Have I not chosen you?" [40]

Questions to Meditate On
Do you know what God's will is for *your* life?
Are you carrying out God's will on a daily basis?
Have you asked God to reveal His purpose for your life?
What is holding you back from doing God's will?

Your Call to Action
Seek God. Learn His plan.
Embrace God's will.

FATHER GOD'S BUSINESS

"Did you not know that I must be about My Father's business?" [1]

Jesus is a serious businessman. His disciples are businessmen, -women, and -children carrying out Father God's will. When Jesus's own parents confronted Him about His whereabouts, His response was: *"Did you not know that I must be about My Father's business?"* [2] His priority, focus, and primary desire was to do the will of the Father. He understood God's will. He knew His purpose. He carried out His mission. He was obedient.

In order to successfully carry out Father God's will, you need to first understand Father God's business. Do you understand His business plan? Have you studied the design, vision, mission, and the end product and service it produces? Jesus understands His Father's business. He knows exactly how it works.

Jesus explained how His Father's business works in His parables. Father God's business is referred to in the Scriptures as *The Kingdom of Heaven.* The business has several departments including legal, accounting, sales, investments, and even a farming division.

Father God's fields produce a harvest of His righteous people. His services are free of charge and non-refundable, and the end product is backed by a beyond-lifetime warranty with an eternal guarantee. Jesus is personally on the assembly line sorting out the end products for permanent distribution.

"When the Son of Man comes in his glory, and all angels with him, He will sit on his glorious throne. All the nations will be

gathered before him, and he will separate the people one from an-
other as a shepherd separates the sheep from the goats. He will put
the sheep on his right and the goats on his left. Then the King will
say to those on his right, 'Come, you who are blessed by my father;
take your inheritance, the kingdom prepared for you since the cre-
ation of the world.' " [3]

Father God is in business to be profitable. He has a zero-tolerance
policy for employees who do not produce income. Let's take a look at
how the investment department operates as described in the parable of
the talents.

"The Kingdom of Heaven can be illustrated by the story of a man
going on a long trip. He called together his servants and entrusted
his money to them while he was gone. He gave five bags of silver to
one, two bags of silver to another, and one bag of silver to the last—
dividing it in proportion to their abilities. He then left on his trip.

*"The servant who received the five bags of silver **began to invest***
the money and earned five more. The servant with two bags of sil-
*ver also **went to work** and earned two more. But the servant who*
received the one bag of silver dug a hole in the ground and hid the
master's money.

"After a long time their master returned from his trip and called
them to give an account of how they had used his money. The ser-
vant to whom he had entrusted the five bags of silver came forward
with five more ...

"The master was full of praise. 'Well done, my good and faithful
servant.' ...

"The servant who had received the two bags of silver came forward
...

"The master said, 'Well done, my good and faithful servant.' ...

"*Then the servant with the one bag of silver came and said, '… I was afraid I would lose your money, so I hid it in the earth. Look, here is your money back.'*

"*But the master replied, 'You wicked and lazy servant! … why didn't you deposit my money in the bank? At least I could have gotten some interest on it.'*

"*Then he ordered, 'Take the money from this servant, and give it to the one with the ten bags of silver. To those who use well what they are given, even more will be given, and they will have an abundance. But from those who do nothing, even what little they have will be taken away.'*" [4]

The legal agreements in Father God's business are the covenants with mankind and have become the bylaws of time. Every time we write or type the date, we are reminded of Christ's legal authority in this world.

"*But this is the covenant that I will make with the house of Is-rael after those days, says the LORD: I will put My law in their minds, and write it on their hearts; and I will be their God, and they shall be My people. No more shall every man teach his neigh-bor, and every man his brother, saying, 'Know the LORD,' for they all shall know Me, from the least of them to the greatest of them, says the LORD. For I will forgive their iniquity, and their sin I will remember no more.*" [5]

The sales department is composed of "fishers of men." This is how Jesus runs the sales team.

"*The Kingdom of Heaven is like a fishing net that was thrown into the water and caught fish of every kind. When the net was full, they dragged it up onto the shore, sat down, and sorted the good fish into crates, but threw the bad ones away. That is the way it will be at the end of the world. The angels will come and separate the wicked people from the righteous.*" [6]

Father God runs a tight ship. His farming division is especially shrewd with its employees, serious about quality control. Here is what Jesus does with the employees who choose not to follow His policies.

> *"The kingdom of heaven is like a man who sowed good seed in his field. But while everyone was sleeping, his enemy came and sowed weeds among the wheat, and went away. When the wheat sprouted and formed heads, then the weeds also appeared. …*
>
> *"The servants asked him, 'Do you want us to go and pull them up?'*
>
> *"'No,' he answered, 'because while you are pulling the weeds, you may uproot the wheat with them. Let both grow together until the harvest. At that time I will tell the harvesters: First collect the weeds and tie them in bundles to be burned; then gather the wheat and bring it into my barn.'"* 7

The accounting department sweats the details. Accounts receivable expects to collect the check. The employees of Father God's business are prudent. His managers do not waste resources, as seen in this parable about a rich man who fired his manager because of waste.

> *"The manager said to himself, 'What shall I do now? My master is taking away my job. I'm not strong enough to dig, and I'm ashamed to beg—I know what I'll do so that, when I lose my job here, people will welcome me into their houses.'*
>
> *"So he called in each one of his master's debtors. He asked the first, 'How much do you owe my master?'*
>
> *"'Nine hundred gallons of olive oil,' he replied.*
>
> *"The manager told him, 'Take your bill, sit down quickly, and make it four hundred and fifty.' …*
>
> *"The master commended the dishonest manager because he had acted shrewdly. … I tell you, use worldly wealth to gain friends for yourselves, so that when it is gone, you will be welcomed into eternal dwellings.*

"Whoever can be trusted with very little can also be trusted with much, and whoever is dishonest with very little will also be dishonest with much. So if you have not been trustworthy in handling worldly wealth, who will trust you with true riches? And if you have not been trustworthy with someone else's property, who will give you property of your own?" [8]

Put your future security in God's hands to safeguard your life. When you invest in Father God's business, regardless of your timing or economic circumstances, your investment is secure. Father God's business is never going to fail. It has not failed since the beginning of time. The Bible continues to be the bestselling book of all time. Why is that? Because the principles ring true generation after generation, regardless of the season, regardless of the era. The Bible's principles are tried and true. They work. If you align yourself with Father God's business and you put your future security within His future security, your future is safe and sound. If you place your future in the hands of a worldly company or the security of a stock or a bond or some piece of real estate, you will be greatly disappointed over the long term. As the Scripture says, *Cast but a glance at riches, and they are gone, for they will surely sprout wings and fly off to the sky like an eagle.* [9]

Why would you want to bet your future on things that are speculative? Things that could potentially fall apart at any moment? You have a guaranteed retirement plan, guaranteed success with all the benefits you could ever desire in Father God's business. Invest your time and energy being a great employee of Father God's business. It's the best corporation to work for on Planet Earth.

Decide to serve Father God with all of your heart. Serving your employer and loving your boss can be challenging. If you work for an ethical company, *answering to your boss* represents *doing the right thing.* As an employee, you are tempted to do what *you* want to do and hope that you don't get caught. If you truly love the Lord, serve Him as your boss. There's nothing more frustrating for an employer than to pour out love, care, and attention on an employee who undervalues or discounts those benefits. This is the same way that the Lord feels if He pours out His love and attention to His children yet they ignore Him, reject Him, or walk away. How can God conduct His business with employees like that?

Remember, Jesus is a *serious* businessman. He *is here* through His Holy Spirit and continues to manage His Father's business. Right before Jesus returned to heaven, He asked God to send us the Holy Spirit, the Spirit of truth, to help us conduct Father God's business here on earth.

"If you love me, keep my commands. And I will ask the Father, and he will give you another advocate to help you and be with you forever—the Spirit of truth ... Before long, the world will not see me anymore, but you will see me. Because I live, you also will live. On that day you will realize that I am in my Father, and you are in me, and I am in you." [10]

Love the Lord. He has always loved you. By loving the Lord with all of your heart, you are metaphorically raising your hand to advance your position within His company. In essence, you are asking for a promotion. Through devotion, you are requesting a leadership opportunity. The corporate ladder is reversed within Father God's business. The last comes first. So in order to move higher in Father God's business, you need to go lower. You need to disciple others; you need to serve and love others more than you are serving and loving yourself. This is Father God's business model. At the heart of His operations, Father God's business is operated by the fruit of the Spirit based on biblical beliefs.

Love the things that God loves. When you value the things that God values, you will be an essential asset to the business. By diving deep into the core values, learning the biblical beliefs, and exercising those biblical beliefs on a daily basis, you start to disciple and inspire others within the business to want to follow your lead. When others see the results in your life—the benefits that you are receiving from working for Father God's business—they are motivated to want to work for Father God's business as well.

If you've ever known anyone who's worked at a great company and they talk about how wonderful their work is, the first question that pops in your mind is *"How do I get a job there?"* The good news is there's plenty of employment opportunities available at Father God's business. Regardless of the economy or unemployment situation anywhere else in the world, Father God's business is always open for business and is constantly hiring. Father God's business does not fire people. They quit or give up.

Father God's business molds, shapes, and nurtures the employees' characters so that they can go out and conduct God's will. There's no need for any insurance policies because God Himself is the ultimate insurance policy. The payroll is on time every time, never misses a beat, and provides exactly enough wages to take care of the needs of the employees. Instead of investing in stocks, bonds, or any other type of worldly asset, the 401(k) plan invests into heavenly investments like Bible translation and other godly missions that carry eternal value.

God will protect those who are loyal to Him. Just like an employer will protect his employees who are loyal to him, God has a vested interest in making sure that His employees are well taken care of. He wants them to rest. He wants them to have a wonderful family life. He wants them to vacation and take time off, to enjoy other hobbies in their lives. God is a magnificent boss and one *you want to work for*. But until you put down your own passions and desires as a *freelancer* and decide that you're going to be a dedicated employee of Father God's business, you will not be able to enjoy any of the company's benefits.

Love the LORD, all his faithful people!
The LORD preserves those who are true to him,
but the proud he pays back in full. [11]

When it comes to recruiting, God continually broadcasts His message and provides equal employment opportunities. He will never force you into His organization. God's recruiting message is one of love that draws you in. He sends different recruiters at different seasons in your life to give you the opportunity to join the company over and over again. Father God's business has different divisions, different missions—it's multifaceted. You have the opportunity to change departments if your heart desires. When you have been loyal to Him in the little things, He will put you in charge of the big things. God will never betray you.

Mission Principle 4
Father God's business is more important than
your *busyness*.

PATH TO PROGRESS

Desire for your future to be in God's hands. *Psalm 31:15*
Choose to love the Lord. *Psalm 31:23*
Decide that His way is flawless. *Psalm 18:30*
The **result** is God protects you if you are faithful to Him. *Psalm 31:23*
The **promise** is all people belong to God. *Psalm 24:1*

Question from Jesus
"Did you not know that I must be about My Father's business?" [12]

Questions to Meditate On
Are you treating God's business as *serious* business?
Do you have a sense of urgency to carry out Father God's business plan?
How would you rate yourself as a kingdom of heaven employee?
Is your *busyness* taking priority over God's business?

Your Call to Action
Get to work. No excuses.
Play your role. Expand Father God's business.

MISSION FINDER STORY
ONE FLIGHT FROM HEAVEN'S DOOR

For many years, I spent the majority of my summers in the Greek islands. After spending one summer in Santorini, I was on my flight home from Athens to Los Angeles, connecting through London. It was a few years after 9/11, so airport security was still tight and anxiety was still in the air.

As we approached London, the plane suddenly did a U-turn, heading back toward Athens. Perplexed, the other passengers and I stared at each other, waiting for the pilot to come on the loudspeaker, hopefully with news other than that we were headed for a crash landing. If you've ever been in a Boeing 747 that makes a sharp U-turn, believe me, you feel it. The pilot announced that we would be returning to Athens even though we were hours into our flight and just getting ready to descend on London. There weren't many details other than there was a threat at the London airport and we needed to return to Athens.

Upon arriving in Athens, we were greeted by news cameras, reporters, and people questioning the details of our flight. Within moments, we were informed that twenty terrorists had been apprehended before boarding flights headed to major cities in America including Los Angeles. [1] There is no doubt one of the arrested terrorists would have been on my connecting flight from London to Los Angeles, which was on a major carrier. I believe God spared my life that day and many others' lives. I'm eternally grateful to Scotland Yard, which arrested those terrorists and foiled their plan.

It was utter chaos in the Athens airport; everyone was frantic, trying to get on the next flight home. The FAA had grounded all planes in Europe and in America. Yet everyone was still scrambling to try to get home. The lines to the ticket counter were tremendous. I paused for a moment, then decided to take a different approach. Rather than fight the crowd trying to fly through multiple European cities to try to get back home days later, I decided to look at this situation as a sign that it was time for me to spend some alone time reflecting on the purpose of my life. I went to a ticket counter with no one in line, a local Greek airline. I booked the first ticket back to Santorini for a week until things cooled down. I was about to discover God's will for my life.

I remember flying back to Santorini with a new perspective on my life, a new understanding of just how fragile and precious life is, and how quickly things can change in your life in a moment. All my worldly attachments seemed less important. On the flight back to Santorini, I made a new friend. A Swiss man was returning to his vacation home in Santorini to get it prepared for sale. I shared my experience in real estate and offered to assist him with the preparations and marketing. He was very empathetic to my situation given the terrorist arrests in London, and he offered to host me for the week, a very generous offer.

Upon arrival, I discovered his *vacation home* was better described as a first-class waterfront estate overlooking Santorini's picturesque Caldera. The location was magnificent. Quite possibly the most spectacular view I have ever seen from a private residence in the world. The home was ultimately sold to a five-star boutique hotel. I revisit this landmark in my life whenever I return to the island.

The next seven days put a new perspective on my life, my path, and my faith. It is a moment in my life that I've come to realize God's hand was all over. He was protecting me, then revealing to me that there was more to my life. He had a destiny ready for me to unfold and a mission waiting for me to complete. It was my wake-up call. No more delaying my destiny. Over the next few years, I surrendered my life to Christ. Soon after, I was married. My family and business flourished. I made a *choice* to commit all of my time and energy toward seeking God's will. I made a *decision* to invest my time, talent, and treasure toward seeking eternal treasures. This was the beginning of my journey to find and fulfill God's will for my life.

step two

CLARIFY YOUR VISION

WHAT DOES GOD SEE IN YOU?

SEE THE BIG PICTURE

Where there is no vision, the people perish. [1]

What does God see in every one of His children? Potential. Opportunity. The potential for you to thrive. The opportunity for you to impact others around you with your love through His love for you. The best way to understand God's vision for His children is to think about your vision for your children. If you don't have children, imagine your vision for someone you love deeply who is younger than you. What do you desire for them? If you truly love them, you desire blessing and well-being. God desires the same for you.

How do you have vision? What steps are necessary in order to *receive* vision?

1. Desire the **impartation**. Ask God in prayer.
2. Focus through **meditation**. No distractions.
3. Receive holy **visualization**. Be still.

Noise, distractions, and interruptions are the enemy of a creative imagination. Vision starts with your desire. Start to believe you are capable of *having* visions. Your intimacy and relationship with God will determine the vision He will impart in your heart. Ever wonder how all of a sudden you thought of something that turned out to be a great idea? That's the Holy Spirit placing a vision into your heart. Big or small, the Holy Spirit reveals them all. The greatest inventions of all time throughout mankind have come from an instant moment of clarification.

In order to clarify your vision, you need to have a vision to clarify. In order to successfully carry out *your mission*, you will need to clearly understand what the objective is. What are you aiming for? For many, visions do not come naturally. Clearly seeing into the foreseeable future may be a challenge for you. If visions do not come naturally, it may feel foreign or frustrating trying to imagine what you are supposed to be doing with your life. When you understand God's vision for your life, you will be able to apply His vision to your circumstances. In turn, this will set your mission in motion within the context of your life. So what exactly is God's vision for you?

The Lord's Prayer helps you clarify God's primary vision for your life as it states: "*Our Father in heaven, / hallowed be Your name, / Your kingdom come. Your will be done, / on Earth as it is in heaven.*" [2] So it's clear that establishing attributes of the kingdom of heaven here on earth is God's will and *His vision* for every believer.

The key to clarity is obedience. How can you apply "establishing the kingdom of heaven" and "transforming into the image of Christ" into your own life to help clarify your vision and fulfill the mission God has for you? Obedience. When you are obedient to God's Word, you will receive clear and undistorted vision to light your path and guide your way. When you are disobedient to God's Word, your vision is unclear. Your decisions become flawed. Your judgments are not sound. In your heart, you know of your own disobedience. It reminds you with feelings of guilt, shame, and discontent once the behavior is complete. Repenting and turning 180 degrees in the other direction is how to recalibrate your mind and receive clear, undistorted vision.

Our best example of clear vision is Christ Himself. He foresaw the events that will come to pass. **What did Jesus promise you? What was His vision for *your* future?**

- Jesus promised to come back. [3]
- Jesus will prepare a place for you. [4]
- Jesus will return when least expected. [5]

- Jesus will not abandon you as an orphan. [6]
- When everything is prepared, Jesus will come back for you. [7]
- The servants who are prepared as they await His return will get a reward. [8]
- Some people will be left and some people will be taken at the rapture. [9]
- There's plenty of room in the Father's house. [10]
- Those who believe without seeing Jesus are blessed. [11]
- Just as Jesus lives forever, you will also live forever. [12]

If Jesus were to summarize His vision for the future in a letter to you from heaven, it might read like this:

Brother/Sister,
I have great news to share. Dad showed me the blueprints for the family's future home. There is a place just for you. Remember to share His plans and His truth with your family, friends, colleagues, and everyone around you. We have plenty of room. Who doesn't need a new home and some good news in a time such as this? Spread the word. Dad is working away finalizing His plans for a new heaven and a new earth, which includes your new home. Everything is almost ready. Can't wait to show you; it looks amazing! Be ready. I promise to return soon, when you least expect it, with rewards. Let's help Dad implement the final phase of development. Remember, time is of the essence. See you soon.

Your fellow heir,
Jesus

God instructs you to guard your eyes. The reason is because the inputs that you allow into your eyes will affect the outputs of the vision that He places in your heart. When you guard your eyes, you protect His instructions. When you ignore His instructions, you cannot see His big picture. You start to create your own picture. But there's no need for that. God has already painted and presented a perfect plan. You need to trust Him. That's part of seeing the big picture.

Your decision to trust the Lord will change your life. Once you've decided to dedicate your life to the Lord, you will begin anew. You'll have a life in which there is a new leader, a blueprint to follow, and a destiny to fulfill.

The LORD is my light and my salvation—
whom shall I fear?
The LORD is the stronghold of my life—
of whom shall I be afraid? [13]

When you look at the big picture, look for the light. The light at the end of the tunnel, the light that shines bright to conquer all darkness. That light is Jesus. Do not seek the things of this world that provide a false sense of security, happiness, or protection. Instead, desire the Lord to be your light and your salvation. It is through His light that you will shine the brightest.

As Jesus came to save others, you will be used as an instrument of His to rescue others. You will have the opportunity to help others who are trapped in bondage and slaves to sin. By providing Scripture and wisdom, you will be able to set them free by helping them to break chains in their lives and overcome obstacles. You can do this by sharing your testimony about what God has done in your life, how He has transformed your heart, and how His blessings have been poured out through your obedience to Him. People are attracted to His light. You are instructed to shine bright, the same way Jesus did when He walked on earth.

"Let your light so shine before men, that they may see your good works and glorify your Father in heaven." [14]

Deep in everyone's heart there is a desire for salvation. Humans need to be rescued. Our life and time on this unstable earth are finite. People are seeking something concrete, reliable, guaranteed, solid as a rock. Something that overcomes the darkness that looms. If you've accepted Jesus, you know that He is the answer. You know that He is the hope and the light in salvation.

The *big picture* for followers of Jesus is to learn how to spread His light and share His salvation worldwide. There's no better time than the present day, during the digital information age, that allows you to distribute lots of light quickly from one end of the globe to the other. Use your creativity as you exercise your God-given talents to express what God has done for you. Share His light with others through unique ways that draw people toward Him. Present compelling questions that make people question their own salvation.

Imagination and creativity are within you. If you want to *see the big picture*, you need to make sure that you're looking through the right lens. Ask God to unleash the creativity and imagination in your heart so that you can see through His lens and further His purposes. Remember, your vision is not your mission. Your vision is the end game. Your mission is how you get there. In other words, your vision is *what* you are trying to accomplish and your mission is *how* you plan to accomplish it. For most, task-driven missions are much easier to comprehend than imagination-driven visions.

Imagine the end. Your last breath. What does that look like for you? Once your vision is established, the next step is to lay the groundwork to discover, plan, and carry out your mission.

Mission Principle 5
God's vision for your life is to establish the
kingdom of heaven.

Path to Progress

Desire for God to cleanse you from your unseen faults. *Psalm 19:12*
Choose to guard God's instructions as you shield your eyes. *Proverbs 7:2*
Decide to trust God. *Psalm 4:5*
The **result** is when you are righteous, you will see God. *Psalm 17:15*
The **promise** is God's favor lasts through your lifetime. *Psalm 30:5*

Question from Jesus
"Why are you troubled, and why do doubts rise in your minds?" [15]

Questions to Meditate On
What do you believe is God's vision for you?
What do you want to accomplish in your life?
Are doubts clouding your vision?
Do you see yourself as a child in God's eyes?

Your Call to Action
Start small. Dream big.
Clarify your vision. See the big picture.

SHAPE YOUR VISION

"Seek the Kingdom of God above all else, and live righteously, and he will give you everything you need." [1]

Surround yourself in an atmosphere filled with biblical principles and values. This will help shape your vision. What are your natural talents? What ministry is your heart most drawn toward? As the saying goes, "Get in where you fit in." If you do not already know your God-given talents, an assessment may be necessary to help you identify your natural and spiritual talents. Scripture reminds us that God has ordained certain gifts for certain people. No one gift is better than the other. Believers worldwide make up the body of Christ here on earth.

He [Jesus] Himself gave some to be apostles, some prophets, some evangelists, and some pastors and teachers, for the equipping of the saints for the work of ministry, for the edifying of the body of Christ. [2]

When you know you've been called to do something, your passion and purpose will overcome you. You're no longer working or doing a job; rather, you are fulfilling your destiny. Let me tell you, it's exciting!

God will bless those who bless Him. How do you bless God? You follow His commands. You love His son. You love others. If you find yourself mission-less or find yourself wondering why things aren't working out in your favor, what do you do? Immersing yourself in God's Word is a great place to start. Think of it like a treasure hunt for your purpose. Only you can discover your true purpose within the hidden treasures of the Bible. Your vision of the destination helps you pave the path of your mission. What is driving you? Fear, worry, greed, need for attention? Or is it joy, peace, contentment, and fulfillment?

What are the basic ways to shape your vision? Regardless of your gifts and talents, *your vision* should be based on biblical principles. *Your mission* at its most foundational level is to serve the Lord your God with all your heart, mind, body, and soul. **Your mission is to disciple others. Your mission is to love others. Your mission is to teach others God's Word. Your mission is to baptize others.** If you build *your vision* based upon these biblical mission principles, you can rest assured you will stay in God's will. Some basic actions to help you shape your vision and find your niche are:

1. Ask
2. Listen
3. Receive instruction
4. Do it
5. Repeat

A good friend of mine streamlines it even further and often reminds me, "Plan. Do. Review."

Trust in the LORD and do good. [3]

Shape your vision around doing good. Desire to trust in the Lord, and He will help you shape your vision. He will show you a picture of what *doing good* looks like from His perspective. God's divine design is for you to love others and to love Him, so any vision that comes from heaven will include those activities. This could be through faith; this could be through mercy; this could be through justice; it could be through generosity. Whatever vision God places on your heart, you know it came from above if the cornerstone of the vision is to *do good.*

Trust that the Lord will help you figure out all the pieces and parts that you need to achieve the vision. What is something that pulls at your heart that would: benefit fellow human beings, society as a whole, or the planet on which you live? Make sure your vision is aligned with Father God's business and His business plan, which is to share His son, Jesus Christ, with the entire world. Include the Holy Spirit. Then, simply trust God. Trust that He will provide everything you need in order to carry out that vision.

Be still before the LORD
and wait patiently for him. [4]

As you start to shape your vision, it is important to be still, to be quiet, to invite the presence of the Holy Spirit into your life to help you shape that vision. God instructs you to go behind closed doors, to be still and listen, and to seek refuge when you pray.

"But when you pray, go into your room, close the door and pray to your Father, who is unseen. Then your Father, who sees what is done in secret, will reward you." [5]

Listen more than you talk. Do not act hastily. Seek wise counsel if you are unsure. Create an environment that invites the Holy Spirit's presence into your life. Be deliberate about setting up a space that allows for your eyes and ears to be opened. Wait patiently for God to lead you. Just because God is giving you a vision this season doesn't mean the vision is going to come to reality during this season. Many of the visions I have received in my life have come to fruition years later. Some visions I received took a decade or more to come to pass. Meanwhile, God matures us along the way.

"Write down the revelation
and make it plain on tablets
so that a herald may run with it.
For the revelation awaits an appointed time; it speaks of the end
and will not prove false.
Though it linger, wait for it;
it will certainly come
and will not delay." [6]

Once the initial seed is planted, God shapes that vision over and over throughout the years until the vision becomes a reality. Patience is key. Spending time in His presence, seeking Him, and being still as He shapes the vision are part of the journey. Remember, God is the potter, you are the clay. Don't get in the way as He shapes. That's what He does best.

Yet you, LORD, are our Father.
We are the clay, you are the potter;
we are all the work of your hand. [7]

What was Jesus's niche while He was here on earth? He paints that picture when He shares with us: "*For I have come down from heaven not to do my will but to do the will of him who sent me. And this is the will of him who sent me, that I shall lose none of all those he has given me, but raise them up at the last day. For my Father's will is that everyone who looks to the Son and believes in him shall have eternal life, and I will raise them up at the last day.*" [8]

Jesus clearly articulates God's will for His life. He found His niche. How do you know if your vision or your niche is really God's will for your life? How can you tell?

Look at the fruit of your life. A heavenly definition of *fruit* is the off-spring from the tree of your life. If there is visible, healthy, abundant fruit surrounding you, then you can be confident you are in the midst of God's will. If there is no visible fruit, or there's spoiled fruit, you may need to consider replanting with fresh vision and a godly mission. There are obstacles or roadblocks preventing you from breaking the chains that are holding you back.

The next step is to learn how to identify those roadblocks, overcome them, and break the chains that hold you back from fulfilling God's will.

Mission Principle 6
Shape your vision with biblical principles and values.

Day 6

Path to Progress

Desire to trust in God and do good things. *Psalm 37:3*
Choose to be still in God's presence. *Psalm 37:7*
Decide that with God you can climb any wall. *Psalm 18:29*
The **result** is you will lie down and sleep peacefully. *Psalm 4:8*
The **promise** is God lights a lamp for you. *Psalm 18:28*

Question from Jesus
"What do you want me to do for you?" [9]

Questions to Meditate On
What does my last breath on earth look like?
Have I asked God to show me His vision for my life?
Am I running away from God's vision for my life?
Who or what can help me clarify my vision?

Your Call to Action
Desire revelation. Seek the Lord.
Pray for clarity. Shape your vision.

SPOT ROADBLOCKS AHEAD

"Here on earth you will have many trials and sorrows." [1]

Roadblocks to your success take form as idols in your heart. Roadblocks to anticipate on your journey to clarify your vision include doubt, fear, apathy, and disobedience. Let's explore how to overcome them.

Doubt and faith cannot coexist. You cannot serve two masters.

"No one can serve two masters. Either you will hate the one and love the other, or you will be devoted to the one and despise the other. You cannot serve both God and money." [2]

Just like you cannot serve God and money, you need to choose between submitting to a life rich in faith or conceding to a life full of doubt. Doubt will cloud your vision. Doubt will stimulate uncertainty in your ability to carry out your mission. Doubt is a liar. It is the root of deception. **When in doubt, read Scripture.**

"That is why I tell you not to worry about everyday life." [3]

One of my favorite definitions of **fear** is **f**alse **e**xpectations **a**ppearing **r**eal. Circumstances and moments of hardship can create the illusion of despair. At some point in life, we have all felt some level of depression. During an intense moment, we can all become fearful. This is normal. But living a life full of fear will only result in a life full of uncertainty and discontent. Do not let fear or doubt paralyze you. It's no more than a roadblock attempting to stop you from carrying out God's will, trying to prevent you from fulfilling your destiny.

"I have told you this so that my joy may be in you and that your joy may be complete." [4]

Joy, on the other hand, overrules fear and depression. Joy-focused people look for the silver lining. Deep rooted joy goes above and beyond temporary satisfaction. Joy resides in a special place in your heart. It gives you a continual smile and stable contentment.

Oh, the joys of those who do not
follow the advice of the wicked,
or stand around with sinners,
or join in with mockers. [5]

Happiness is not joy. Joy stands in a category of its own. Happiness is temporary; joy is eternal. Choosing to be joyful, despite what surrounds you, will lift your spirit and that of others in your presence. No one can steal your joy when you have *the joy of the Lord.* Temporary setbacks and life circumstances may cause momentary unhappiness, but underneath it all resides everlasting joy. This joy comes from the promises the Lord has made. If you embrace that element of joy, you can go through any obstacle that life presents you. This type of joy in your life will conquer temporary setbacks and life circumstances that come your way. You need to study joy and understand what true joy looks like and how to find it. God explains through His Scripture the ability to discover joy through love.

Your love has given me much joy and comfort, my brother, for your kindness has often refreshed the hearts of God's people. [6]

Joy motivates you to do things even when you don't feel like it. Motivational speakers attempt to inspire and bring joy to others. They speak with confidence, conviction, aspiration, and direction in the world's terms. But the joy often fizzles once the teaching is over. Why is that?

Because excitement, entertainment, and inspiration do not create true joy. However, an individual who embraces the Holy Spirit brings joy to the room through hope and faith. Joy is the fuel you need to accomplish your vision.

Each day we put fuel into the engine of life. Is it clean energy leading you to a safe, secure destination or dirty fuel leading to a rough road filled with potholes and headed toward an unknown destination? Within the engine of life, your heart is the gas tank. It can be completely full, three-quarters of the way full, half full, a quarter tank, or completely empty. God dispenses the gasoline of joy into your heart. When you're walking in His will, clarifying your vision, and seeking His will, He will fill the gas tank of your heart with joy.

"I have loved you even as the Father has loved me. Remain in my love. When you obey my commandments, you remain in my love, just as I obey my Father's commandments and remain in his love. I have told you these things so that you will be filled with my joy. Yes, your joy will overflow!" [7]

An extra benefit of following the Father's commandments is that we continue to pump joy into the air pockets of our hearts. One more way that joy can be a mainstay in our hearts is by us being obedient. Jesus was clear when He said, *"You are my friends **if** you do what I command."* [8]

Surely, LORD, you bless the righteous;
you surround them with your favor as with a shield. [9]

God promises to put a shield around you to protect you from the things that would try to rid you of your joy. When joy can be developed into a daily habit with God's shield of protection, you will be a force to be reckoned with. Any vision or mission you set your mind to—that is biblically based and aligned with God's will—is designed from inception to be accomplished. Be prepared for others to slander and persecute you because of the joy in your faith. Also be prepared for God to give you the conviction, strength, courage, and boldness to endure verbal or physical persecution as it comes. Know that by serving God in the face of adversity, you are joining in a long line of prophets, saints, and other highly respected and favored citizens of the kingdom of heaven.

"God blesses you when people mock you and persecute you and lie about you and say all sorts of evil things against you because you are my followers. Be happy about it! Be very glad! For a great reward awaits you in heaven. And remember, the ancient prophets were persecuted in the same way." [10]

Combat selfishness with generosity. It's the only medicine that does the trick. Throughout your mission, you will be asked to give everything to fulfill your mission. To give of your time, your attention, your talent, and your financial resources. Don't stop giving. Give until you have nothing left to give.

"Your gift will return to you in full—pressed down, shaken together to make room for more, running over, and poured into your lap. The amount you give will determine the amount you get back." [11]

Jesus has promised you that the amount you give will determine the amount you will get back. He promised that your gifts will return to you in full. It's when you become insular, when you retain or stockpile your gifts or financial resources, that you create problems, obstacles, and roadblocks for yourself on your path to progress.

Stockpiling assets confirms you are not completely trusting in God. If He has promised that your gift will return in full and how much you give will determine how much you get back, it's evident you need to give as much as possible in order to receive as much as possible. There's a popular expression in the Christian world that goes like this: "You can't out-give God."

I said that once to a friend of mine's father, and he immediately said to me, "Have you ever tried?" I paused when he said this, thought for a moment, and realized, "No, I've never tried to out-give God. I should give that a shot." [12] My friend's father knows a thing or two about giving and living a life of generosity. His name is David Green. He is the founder of Hobby Lobby and a self-made billionaire. He has given away more than $500 million in his lifetime and continues to give millions on an annual basis. [13] He is one of my heroes.

The entire Green family has been an inspirational, model example of what complete trust in God looks like with your finances. They accept God at His word that the amount you give will determine the amount that you get back. Any gift that you give will be returned to you in full.

Everyday generosity is part of my life. I love giving. However, throughout my journey of generosity, I've discovered something more near and dear to Christ's heart.

"What sorrow awaits you teachers of religious law and you Pharisees. Hypocrites! For you are careful to tithe even the tiniest income from your herb gardens, but you ignore the more important aspects of the law—justice, mercy, and faith. You should tithe, yes, but do not neglect the more important things." [14]

Do justice, mercy, and faith supersede generosity? Admittedly, we have all been apathetic to certain injustices in the world. But the world at large is raising their hands and saying, "Things aren't right! Things aren't *just*." How do we fix this? Politics aside, the majority of humans share an interest in justice, mercy, and faith. If you desire God's blessing, you need to seek faith, thirst for mercy, and hunger for justice.

"God blesses those who hunger and thirst for justice,
for they will be satisfied." [15]

If you feel mission-less or uncertain about God's call on your life, you are not alone. The fact is many people have yet to discover their callings. At the same time, there are enough injustices in this world to keep you busy for a hundred lifetimes. Anyone claiming there's nothing to do or to get involved with to carry out God's will on earth is living in denial. Simply turn on the news, scroll through social media, or flip through the newspaper. You can identify an injustice in a heartbeat that needs someone to stand in the gap, shine bright, speak up, and claim victory over that injustice. Be that light today.

"You are my friends if you do what I command." [16]

Learn to overcome disobedience. To be a friend of Jesus, you must be obedient to His commands. Jesus has a unique friendship with His friends. I listen to my friends, I care about my friends, I love my friends, but I wouldn't say that I'm obedient to my friends. They have their life and world perspective, and I have mine. They make their own decisions and choices. Jesus calls us to a new type of friendship through the gospel. He expects obedience as part of our friendship with Him. Jesus offers a true friendship that encompasses the principle of *forgive and forget.*

Disobedience is tempting. No one likes being told what to do on a consistent basis. In general, humans tend to want to do things their own way. This stubbornness and willfulness separate us from God. Jesus never asks you to do anything that He did not personally do while He was here on earth. He was the model example when it came to obedience. He followed His Father's commandments. He didn't try to bend the rules. He was clear on who His number one was.

Learn to spot the roadblocks. The greatest risk to any proclaimed Christian today is to go on with life believing they are saved only to arrive at heaven's door to hear Jesus say, "Get away from me. I never knew you." [17]

Satan, the prince of the air, happens to also be the prince of the airwaves where most modern communication flows. Whether it's internet signals, cell phone towers, satellites, radio waves, or any other form of broadcasting, it travels through the air and is subject to frequencies being manipulated, regulated, or just miscommunicated. The majority of the content we digest today directly into our hearts and minds (primary inputs) is unhealthy and directly affects our thoughts and behaviors (primary outputs). Spot the roadblocks in your life today. Choose new inputs to express new outputs.

For the LORD watches over the path of the godly,
but the path of the wicked leads to destruction. [18]

When you follow God's commandments, He will watch over you. He has a vested interest in keeping you safe. You are carrying out *His* will for *His* kingdom. God will keep you here as long as *He* needs you here. If He wants you home, He will bring you home. If you could see heaven, you'd want to be there. However, just like Jesus, you are here to do *His* will, not your own will.

Consider it pure joy, my brothers and sisters, whenever you face trials of many *kinds, because you know that the testing of your faith produces perseverance.* [19]

Mission Principle 7
You can overcome *anything* when Christ is your Lord and Master.

PATH TO PROGRESS

Desire joy in your life. *Psalm 1:1*
Choose not to be afraid, knowing God is close beside you. *Psalm 23:4*
Decide that God will protect you and comfort you. *Psalm 23:4*
The **result** is you will have greater joy than those abundant in harvest and wine. *Psalm 4:7*
The **promise** is the Lord watches over your path if you're godly.
Psalm 1:6

Question from Jesus
"Do you want to get well?" [20]

Questions to Meditate On
What are the roadblocks in your life?
How do you plan to overcome those roadblocks?
What are some of the doubts and fears in your life?
What selfish habits do you need to change?

Your Call to Action
Ignore doubt and fear. Become selfless.
Overcome obstacles. Spot the roadblocks.

BREAK YOUR CHAINS

"Take heart, because I have overcome the world." [1]

Spiritual bondage is a powerful chain to break. Believers in Christ can be bound in spiritual chains in many ways. Denial, temptation, self-reliance, lack of compassion, and doubting God can all hold you back from following His will for your life. We all have second thoughts, concerns, anxiety, and feelings of inadequacy. Even Jesus asked God for a "pass" the night in Gethsemane before He was crucified. He prayed: *"Father, if you are willing, take this cup from me; yet not my will, but yours be done."* [2]

In other words, Jesus prayed: "God, if there is any other way to accomplish your will besides my crucifixion, please give me a way out. If not, I will obey you in sacrificing my life for the sins of this world." His body and His spirit were in disagreement. However, the Holy Spirit had authority over His earthly flesh to overcome the temptation.

Why was this Scripture included in the Bible? I believe it was included to show believers that just as we are tempted, Jesus was tempted, and to show us how to overcome the same flesh we fight. Jesus led by example on how to stand firm. When your call to action arrives and your mission is assigned, remember Christ's words in His warning: *"Not everyone who says to me, 'Lord, Lord' will enter the kingdom of heaven, but only the one who does the will of my Father who is in heaven."* [3]

Stop trying to do it yourself. Human nature, stubbornness, and the fighter within us inspire most of us to want to use our own might and strength to get through life. Admission of inadequacy feels like weakness, but it actually frees us from the chains of self-reliance. In the Bible, David was willing to confess his need to God.

I am sick at heart.
How long, O LORD, until you restore me? [4]

When your heart is weak is actually the best time to reach out to God. The body's physical ailments typically follow the heart's ailments. One of the reasons people have a hard time accepting Jesus Christ as their Savior is because they don't believe they *need* to be rescued. Why do you need salvation if nothing is wrong? If your life is going well … what do you need to be rescued from? You just keep moving forward in ignorance of your bondage. Unfortunately, it's not until life throws you a curveball, like a major health issue or some other emotional crisis, that you realize how fragile you are. It's at moments like these that it becomes clear to people that they need God in their lives.

Embrace God's correction rather than desiring a quick fix to your current circumstance. Many times, prayers start out with a quick-fix-it-ticket request and are sent to God like you're bringing your car in to the mechanic. You think your life needs a quick oil change or broken part replaced, but God wants to provide you a whole new engine through His Holy Spirit. For example, you might pray for provision when you have a bill you can't pay. But God may be wanting to break the ideas and attitudes that keep you in bondage financially to improve your situation for the long term. Yet, your quick-fix-it prayers continue to pour in so you can rush to get back on the road. Instead, embrace God's correction in your life and seek His mercy and compassion.

God has a warm heart. When you seek God's mercy and compassion, you will find your own mercy and compassion toward others begin to flourish. When you start acting merciful and compassionately toward others, God's mercy and compassion abound toward you. The warmer your heart is toward others, the warmer His heart is toward you. The colder your heart is toward others, the more distance you place between yourself and God.

Have mercy on me, O LORD, for I am weak;
O LORD, heal me, for my bones are troubled. [5]

You are living in an earthly body that is dying. When compared to the forces of nature, the climate, even many of the animals, humans' physical bodies don't seem impressive. In comparison to many things, human bodies are actually weak. Yet humans live longer than most species and were given intelligence far more vast than any other species. Humans were given a mind to reason as a gift from God. The ability to reason separates humans from all other species and has given humans their superiority.

You need God's strength. When you acknowledge your weakness, you acknowledge your humanity and need for God. God gave humans dominion over the earth. He gave humans the ability to administrate the things of this earth. Going through life believing that your strength is somehow going to overshadow God's sovereign nature is just plain foolish and leads to bondage. Just taking a breath of air is a reminder of His strength and sovereign power. You depend on His divine design of the planet and its oxygen to work properly. To wake up each day and just function, you need His mercy and grace.

God's strength overpowers your weakness. In God's strength, you were designed and set forth. It was through God's strength that you were given life. You should never be ashamed of your own weakness. Embrace your weakness. Celebrate your weakness because it is through the admission of your weakness that God's strength can manifest itself. By continuing to try to do things in your own strength, you reject God's strength and, therefore, end up in chains and weaker. You may be able to carry on for decades this way, but ultimately something, somehow, someday will afflict your life in a way that reveals how truly weak you are without God's strength. Once you have recognized your weakness, the next step is to turn to the source of your strength.

The beautiful design of God's divine plan is that He will use uncomfortable situations to reveal Himself to you. Through pain, suffering, or moments of breakdown, you can be healed and freed when you submit to Him. You were never meant to carry those burdens on your own. You were designed for His strength to flow through you. You were designed to be dependent on Him, not the other way around.

Turn, LORD, and deliver me;
save me because of your unfailing love. [6]

He loves me, He loves me not. This is how many believers go through life with their relationship with Jesus. If things are going well, Jesus loves me. If things are not going well, *by my own definition*, Jesus doesn't love me. They go on with life thinking they have done something wrong, that they have somehow been disqualified from receiving God's love.

God's love does not fail. God can't love you a little more or a little less than He did yesterday. God is love. Therefore, God's love is absolute and steady. To enjoy the full amount of God's love in your life, you must first decide to believe in God's unfailing love. If in your heart you believe that God's love is partial or that He only loves you when you do certain things, then the chains of doubt will block the flow of love that God wants to pour out on you.

God's love is unconditional. He does not show favoritism. God does not love one individual more than another. However, when you look at two individuals' lives, you may see the presence of God's love is more visible in one's life. Why is that? This is a result of that individual's heart being more intimate and open with God so that individual can receive a more complete portion of God's love versus an individual who has decided God's love can only proportionally be in their life.

The LORD has heard my cry for mercy;
the LORD accepts my prayer. [7]

God is a God of absolute truth. There is a difference between the *absolute truth* and someone's *honest opinion* of what they believe the truth to be. Your version of the truth may be your honest opinion. However, as a good father, God is more focused on *His* absolute truth in your life than *your* honest opinion. Keep this in mind as you seek the absolute truth for your life through prayer.

Away from me, all you who do evil,
for the LORD has heard my weeping. [8]

God hears your cries for help. He sees your tears. Once you are clear on your spiritual chains, this will lead you down a path to seek a solution. How do I fix this? How do I rid myself of selfish desires that lead to nothing eternal, that can only harm me in the long run and prevent me from carrying out God's will? Easy. Follow the instruction manual. It's all been laid out in detail in the Bible. But you need to read it, obey it, and stick to it day in and day out. When reading God's Word on a daily basis and journeying toward freedom, challenges and roadblocks will still show up. For this reason, you need an accountability partner to help you stay consistent in your daily walk with God.

Healthy discipleship is the key to consistently breaking unhealthy chains in your life. There is a reason God sent the disciples out two at a time: to disciple one another and keep each other accountable.

As iron sharpens iron,
so one person sharpens another. [9]

At some point in your life, you have most likely purchased a product that looks great fully assembled on the showroom floor. Then upon arriving home, you find out that it comes in a large box with hundreds of nuts and bolts to be assembled by you. You wondered why it was such a great deal. You now realize the exceptional discount was because of the hours of labor you just signed up for to assemble the product. Your weekend plans just changed. You have two options. Follow the instructions or toss them and try to do it yourself. Naturally, you're tempted to wing it and try to do it on your own. But you quickly realize you need to refer to the instruction manual to make sure you have the right tools. Without the tools to assemble the product, it won't work right. It won't function right in the capacity it was originally designed to operate in.

When you try to reshape your human character with your own strength or to break the spiritual chains in your life with your own might, you quickly discover you do not possess the right tools that you need. You must read the right instruction manual. You may be able to assemble the pieces of your life in some capacity, temporarily, but over the long term, your life will become unstable, start to wobble, and the screws will fall out little by little. Eventually, you will fall apart. You cannot win this battle with your own natural strength. You need supernatural strength to break supernatural spiritual chains. You need the fruit of the Spirit. *The fruit of the Spirit is love, joy, peace, longsuffering, kindness, goodness, faithfulness, gentleness, self-control. Against such there is no law.* [10]

Faith and the fruit of the Spirit will break any chains holding you back from fulfilling God's will.

+ **Faith** overcomes doubt, fear, foolishness.
+ **Love** overcomes hate, anger, resentment.
+ **Joy** overcomes anxiety, worry, despair.
+ **Peace** overcomes conflict, hostility, spite.
+ **Longsuffering** overcomes objections, impatience, complaining.
+ **Kindness** overcomes slander, animosity, meanness.
+ **Goodness** overcomes sin, evil, wickedness.
+ **Faithfulness** overcomes infidelity, dishonesty, immorality.
+ **Gentleness** overcomes harshness, cruelty, cold-heartedness.
+ **Self-control** overcomes disobedience, instability, self-indulgence.

You may feel intimidated by God's instruction manual, the Bible. You may feel unfamiliar with the tool. It may not be easy for you to understand or read. It may look too big or too long. Where do you start? You start by following your leader. His name is Jesus.

Once you overcome roadblocks to your success and break the chains holding you back, you will bring clarity to God's vision for your life. Once you clearly see God's vision for your life, the next step is to learn how to follow your leader.

Mission Principle 8
The fruit of the Spirit will break the chains
of spiritual bondage.

PATH TO PROGRESS

Desire the Lord's compassion to restore your sick heart and restore you.
Psalm 6:3
Choose to acknowledge your weakness. *Psalm 6:2*
Decide to believe in God's unfailing love. *Psalm 6:4*
The **result** is the Lord your God will hear your plea and answer your
prayers. *Psalm 6:9*
The **promise** is God has heard your weeping. *Psalm 6:8*

Question from Jesus
"What do you think about the Christ? Whose Son is He?" [11]

Questions to Meditate On
Do you truly believe God can do anything?
What chains in your life today need to be broken?
What are the chains you have successfully broken in the past?
Which fruit of the Spirit can help you overcome your chains?

Your Call to Action
Admit your struggle. Rely on God's strength.
Accept discipleship. Break your chains.

MISSION FINDER STORY
LOVING ONE BY ONE

A soft heart turns away wrath. My wife possesses this type of soft heart and is one of the most merciful people I have met in my lifetime. In the summer of 2010, we went on a mission trip together in Uganda. I was convinced my wife, who had lived in a Southern California bubble for most of her life, would be shocked, possibly even frozen, by the poverty and the despair that is found in many Third World sub-Saharan countries in Africa. I was so wrong.

On the contrary, she amazed me. Her kindness, thoughtfulness, care for the locals, and presence in the face of adversity and severe poverty were amazing. I saw Mother Teresa in her. The mercy and understanding of her compassion were profound. She lifted up the spirits of all those around her. She brought joy, gladness, and cheer. I, on the other hand, spent most of my time debating who was the best soccer team in the world with the natives because the World Cup was airing that summer.

Growing up with a family from Spain, soccer was the only sport that existed in my household. Although I was allowed to practice and play some other sports from time to time, soccer was the religion of the household. For better or for worse, the Arroyos play to win. There is no second place. Real Madrid was my home team growing up. I follow them passionately. Many of the players were on the Spanish national team in 2010, and while we were in Uganda, the final of the World Cup was taking place. Spain vs. Netherlands. I was able to experience this moment of soccer history during breaks from my daily field work on the mission trip. The night of the final match arrived, and it would be a moment in my life I would never forget.

It was just before midnight when the bombs went off. At first, I thought they were fireworks, but there was something unsettling about the low frequency of the noise. It sounded like thunder. It was halftime, and my team was about to win the World Cup. Spain was beating the Netherlands one to zero. I thought possibly the natives were celebrating Spain's one goal or the potential win. It was so late at night that I finished the game and went to sleep.

Little did I know that the next morning I would wake up to a catastrophe. The sounds that I heard, less than a mile away, were terrorist bombs that killed seventy-four spectators at a restaurant and outdoor rugby club where locals gathered to watch the World Cup soccer match. [1] My wife had eaten lunch across the street from the bomb site the day before. Too close for comfort. We loaded on the bus that morning as local reporters and paperboys flooded the street, pressing newspapers against the windows of the bus with photos of those who had been torn apart by the explosion of the bombs. It was a moment in history I will never forget. The imagery is still as fresh as if it happened yesterday.

Our initial reaction was to abort the mission. After much thought, prayer, and reassurance resting in God's promises of protection, the ministry leaders decided to carry on and complete the mission trip. Praise God for the commitment the ministry Loving One by One displayed, showing the courage to *never give up*. The ministry leaders, Ken and Sherry Roberts, were fearless in the midst of chaos. They stayed committed and continue to carry out God's will to this day serving the locals in Kampala, Uganda.

> *"God blesses those who are merciful,*
> *for they will be shown mercy."* [2]

step three

FOLLOW YOUR LEADER

WHAT DOES GOD WANT YOU TO DO?

FOLLOW JESUS

"Whoever does not take up their cross and follow me is not worthy of me." [1]

To follow Jesus is simply to obey His commands. Not some of His commands but all of them. If you proclaim Him to be your king, remember that His words are not suggestions but instructions. His words are absolute truths.

Jesus had a unique method of communication. Primarily, Jesus did four things when He communicated with others. He made promises, gave commands, told stories, and asked questions. He was direct. He did not give a variety of options. He provided specific instructions. If you accept Jesus's words as the infallible truth and the words of God Himself, then His instructions to you should be accepted no differently than His commandments.

Humans tend to need to be reminded very often of the same things over and over. My wife frequently reminds me of my need to be reminded. She is right. The fact is that I forget. For this reason, Jesus didn't give us one gospel, He gave us four gospels. He didn't instruct us one time to obey Him, He repeated it over and over throughout the Scriptures. *"I have revealed you to the ones you gave me from this world. They were always yours. You gave them to me, and they have kept your word."* [2]

Here are some examples of what Jesus instructed us to do to help protect us from the ways of this world. An extensive list is included in Appendix 1.

- ✦ Follow God's commandments. [3]
- ✦ Store up treasures in heaven. [4]

- ✦ Keep watch and pray, so that you will not give in to temptation. [5]
- ✦ If you listen to Jesus's teachings and obey them, you are wise. [6]
- ✦ To be a true disciple, remain faithful to Jesus's commands. [7]
- ✦ Let your good deeds shine forth for all to see. [8]
- ✦ Give and you will receive. [9]
- ✦ Do as Jesus has done to you. [10]
- ✦ Forgive others and you will be forgiven. [11]
- ✦ You must be born again. [12]
- ✦ Teach new disciples to obey all of Jesus's commands. [13]

Choose your allegiance. God is a jealous God. He expects your allegiance and your devotion when you follow His son, Jesus. To be a follower of Jesus is to keep His Word. The initial disciples kept Jesus's word, were obedient, and followed His instructions. They had the advantage of seeing Jesus demonstrate His teaching in a live setting. They had the advantage of seeing Jesus display the fruit of the Spirit. They had the advantage of watching Jesus's methods to heal the sick and perform miracles. However, they did not have the benefit of the New Testament Scripture, Paul's letters, or the advantage of a well-structured and complete manual for life, the Bible, as their playbook.

Thus you will walk in the ways of the good
and keep to the paths of the righteous. [14]

Following the right role model will lead you down the right path. It is said that you are a product of the five people you spend the most time with. First and foremost, your primary role model should be Jesus Christ. Next, you want to follow individuals who have submitted their lives to Jesus Christ and have a thriving and solid relationship with Him. Learn to follow in the footsteps of others who are more mature in their walk with Christ.

Following the right leader takes discernment. To have the right discernment, you need knowledge and understanding of what character traits to seek that make up a good leader. There are many leaders with good intentions, but their character traits being genuine is question-able if they have not submitted to Jesus Christ. A friend of mine, John Windscheffel, said it best when he said: "You cannot completely trust *any* person; you can only trust Christ *in* a person." The Scripture reinforces this point as it reads: *"It is better to trust in the LORD / Than to put con-fidence in man."* [15] Following the footsteps of leaders who have not sub-mitted to Jesus will only lead you down a path to death and destruction.

"Enter through the narrow gate. For wide is the gate and broad is the road that leads to destruction, and many enter through it. But small is the gate and narrow the road that leads to life, and only a few find it." [16]

Following the right leader is essential for your well-being. Seek peo-ple in your life who have already traveled the path that you are seeking. When you follow someone who is aligned with Christ down a path, you are receiving two benefits. The first benefit is walking on the right path with Christ. The second benefit is walking on a path that's already been paved by someone else who can shed light ahead of you as you make your way. Learning from reputable leaders is important, but learning from the Word of God will always be paramount. Leave your comfort zone today by making a commitment to follow Jesus and be obedient to His instruc-tions in everything that you do.

Mission Principle 9
Follow Jesus to find God's will for your life.

Day 9

PATH TO PROGRESS

Desire God to be your light and salvation. *Psalm 27:1*
Choose to follow the steps of good people. *Proverbs 2:20*
Decide to follow the perfect instructions of the Lord. *Psalm 19:7*
The **result** is that if you are godly, the Lord will bless you, fill you with
joy, and surround you with love like a shield. *Psalm 5:12*
The **promise** is the Lord will protect you. *Psalm 14:6*

Question from Jesus
"Do you understand what I have done for you?" [17]

Questions to Meditate On
Is Jesus number one in your life?
Is your will aligned with Jesus's will?
What prevents you from following Jesus more closely?
How do you define following Jesus?

Your Call to Action
Leave your comfort zone.
Choose your allegiance. Follow Jesus.

ACCEPT MISSION POSSIBLE

"Anything is possible if a person believes." [1]

"Your mission … should you choose to accept it …" We all know these famous words from the *Mission: Impossible* series. The main character, Ethan Hunt, lives a life of faith throughout each *Mission: Impossible* movie. Through thick and thin, with obstacles and roadblocks along the way, he manages to persevere as his faith carries him to the finish line. Although seasons of life can feel like a *Mission: Impossible* movie, Christ reminds us that through Him all things are possible.

When you choose to obey God, you set your mission up to succeed. By obeying Him, you will find God's will for your life. It's through obedience that your mission is revealed. Once God knows that you are committed to obeying His commands daily, He will open the doors and create the opportunity for you to get started with your mission. God is with you every step of the way when you are obedient to His Word.

But Jesus looked at them and said to them, "With men this is impossible, but with God all things are possible." [2]

Anything is possible with God. Just like an obedient child is blessed by a mother and father who recognize obedience and openly reward their child, followers of Jesus are recognized for their obedience and rewarded with missions that fulfill the desires of their hearts.

There's no more satisfying feeling than walking down a path knowing that God is taking you on the adventure of a lifetime. It's just you and Him. The world is your oyster. He knows the way. He's been there before. He knows the perfect place for a pit stop, to take a deep breath and rest. He knows which shortcuts to take and which to avoid. He knows what to do when the path gets rocky. Once the sun goes down and the darkness sets in, He provides reassurance and protection. He knows how to navigate through the valleys. He encourages spending a few extra minutes on the mountain tops. He knows the best route, and He is with you every step of *the Way*.

God chose to refer to Himself as a father to illustrate something you could relate to as a human being. God represents the ideal relationship between a father and a child. This vital relationship is the nucleus for your mission. It's the control center. The healthier the nucleus, the stronger the cell. When your relationship is intact with your heavenly Father, when you are obedient to His commands, He is able to do things through you that you never fathomed were possible. He's able to relieve the doubt, alleviate your fears, and show you that your mission is *possible*.

The next step is for you to accept your mission even if you don't feel that you are equipped for that mission. If God is with you, who can be against you?

If God is for us, who can be against us? ³

The master of the universe, the creator of all, opens up and gives you a guarantee that He'll be with you on the journey. That's an incredible insurance policy.

"Be strong and of good courage, do not fear nor be afraid of them; for the LORD your God, He is the One who goes with you. He will not leave you nor forsake you." ⁴

"Your mission" is actually His mission. Accepting *your* mission starts with acknowledging *His* mission. You are the co-pilot, not the pilot. For many, this conviction helps release a lot of unnecessary stress that may go into finding God's will for your life. He will design your mission to align with the desires of your heart. Whatever you have a passion for, whatever tugs at your heart, whatever you are sensitive toward, He will create the opportunity and open the door for you to go through to pursue it.

You were created to *follow* Jesus. You may be called to lead others in your lifetime, but never forget who the commander of the Lord's army is. Your marching orders are to follow your leader, who is Jesus.

When you start your mission, there is so much unknown. It's tempting to start by writing down the tasks and cutting straight to the plan to carry out your mission. I encourage you to spend time with God seeking His presence, asking Him to give you foresight to what this mission looks like at the end. Once a clear vision is established, you won't be able to get it out of your mind. Your heart will race when you think about it. There will be a burning desire inside of you to carry out that mission, to see that vision through to the end. Nothing will be able to stop you. You will wake up in the morning, you will go through your day, and no matter what else you think about, you will come back, front and center, to the mission and vision that God placed on your heart.

Clear vision becomes something you need to express. Vision is something that has been placed *inside of you* that starts to grow *out of you*. Until it's been manifested into the world, you will not be satisfied. That's the type of craving for carrying out God's will that the Lord desires you to have. Something that gets you up in the morning, supercharged. Something that gives you so much joy and purpose you can hardly sleep. Relaxing, hanging out, and even doing recreational activities suddenly lose their luster because you have something much more important at hand. You are working hand in hand with the Creator of the universe to carry out mission *possible*.

As God continues to stir the mission within your heart, it will consume your dreams, and this is where spiritual warfare begins. There will be various distractions, thoughts, and external factors that will try to divert you off your path, but you must stay focused. Remember to recalibrate by reading God's Word and staying in alignment with Him. Write your visions down. Write your missions down. Review them over and over.

It's okay if the vision continues to shape itself over an extended period of time. It is God who directs that vision through your mind and thoughts and weaves the fabric of the mission throughout your body and soul. Remember to use all of your senses—your sight, hearing, touch, smell, taste, your everything—to carry out your mission. Cry out for the vision, and God will deliver. Think of completion points on your journey as pit stops. Celebrate those pit stops. Carrying out your mission does not need to be a grind. Christ promised you that His burden is light.

"Come to Me, all you who labor and are heavy laden, and I will give you rest. Take My yoke upon you and learn from Me, for I am gentle and lowly in heart, and you will find rest for your souls. For My yoke is easy and My burden is light." [5]

When you arrive at a pit stop, praise God, share the testimony, gather a larger group, and point toward the big picture. Share with them the journey from the beginning of the mission to now and how God has faithfully fulfilled that part of the vision. Re-share the vision again and again, and slowly your audience will build. Then it's time to go to the next completion point. Take time to breathe; take a moment to regroup. Restrategize, look at what's working, what's not working, and what needs improvements. Refine the systems, then move forward.

The only thing that makes a mission *impossible* is your acceptance that it is *impossible*. As soon as you convince yourself that you have too much going on in your life or that you're not talented enough—or if your focus is on something else—you have mentally or verbally agreed to cancel the mission. Alternatively, you can open up to the possibility of *mission possible*. By simply recognizing the things in your life that you'll need to delegate or that you need covered to free up your time, you can ask the Holy Spirit for wisdom, knowledge, and understanding of how to prioritize your agenda so that your number one focus can be mission *possible*.

Life can consume you with all types of activities and obligations. Therefore, finding and fulfilling God's mission can get pushed way down the list. Instead of trying to figure it out or waiting until someone drops the mission and vision into your lap, call out to God and ask for help. Consider joining someone else's mission to start with so that you can see that *it's possible*. Learn from others who juggle the same amount of responsibilities as you do but are still carrying out their mission for God.

Give me relief from my distress;
have mercy on me and hear my prayer. [6]

A life-changing season begins with a deep desire in your heart. Without that, you can get stuck in a rut. Excuses or justification will prevent you from proceeding with mission *possible*, and before you know it, that will quickly turn into mission *impossible*. Ever feel like you are tired of being tired? Time keeps on ticking. It's easy to say, "I want my life to improve; I want things to get better," but words and actions are two separate things. Your behaviors and actions are a direct result of your heart's intentions. If you want to have peace, to be safe, and to be free of trouble, what do you need to do in order to achieve those results? Simple. Look at the playbook, follow the instructions, and put together your life with the right assembly kit, the Word of God. Then *accept your mission* and move forward.

Mission Principle 10
Anything is possible with faith in God.

Day 10

Path to Progress

Desire to have better times, to be free of troubles, and to have peace and safety. *Psalm 4:1*
Choose not to get sidetracked. *Proverbs 4:27*
Decide to follow the Lord's righteous commandments. *Psalm 19:8*
The **result** is your plans will succeed if you commit your steps to God. *Proverbs 16:3*
The **promise** is God is with you if you obey Him. *Psalm 14:5*

Question from Jesus
"Why are you so afraid? Do you still have no faith?" [7]

Questions to Meditate On
What is holding you back from doing your mission?
How would you explain your life's mission to a stranger?
Have you been procrastinating or dodging God's calling?
If Jesus returned from heaven today, would you be ready?

Your Call to Action
Fear God only. Don't hesitate.
You can do this. Accept mission possible.

Day 11

STOP DELAYING YOUR DESTINY

Unless the LORD builds the house,
They labor in vain who build it. [1]

A great temptation is to go at life alone. By taking your destiny into your own hands, you have a false sense of control. Your efforts will always be lacking the strength of God, though. You were created for relationships. To listen, to love, to fellowship. When you isolate yourself from the foundational structure of relationships, you isolate yourself from God. In essence, you are delaying your own destiny. That desire for control at the heart of isolation doesn't work out as we intend, as Jesus said: *"If you cling to your life, you will lose it; but if you give up your life for me [Jesus], you will find it."* [2]

Letting go of control in our lives does not come naturally. Sometimes our desire for control manifests as us clinging to worldly attachments. Yet, letting go of those attachments is where true freedom resides. Your earthly life and the things of this world may be all you presently know. Clinging to what you know—whether it's your surroundings, home, family, children, or loved ones—is what feels comfortable. Stepping out in faith—believing there is something beyond what your eyes can see, your ears can hear, or your fingers can touch—takes courage. It takes a willingness to believe in the unseen.

To cling to something is to attempt to control it. Although you may try to control the outcome, you can only attempt to control your circumstances on a daily basis. Although you can't control what comes at you, you can control what comes out of you. You control your responses and reactions. You control what you let in your heart. You control your input and output. Turn your attempt to control your life into freedom through prayer, praise, answers, and fulfillment. They all go hand in hand. The input is through your words of praise and your prayer requests. The result is God's output through His answers and fulfillment toward your praise and prayer requests. Turn your fear of the unknown into your fear of God.

Do you fear God or do you fear things in this world? It can only be one or the other. If you fear God, the fearful things of this world do not alarm you. If the things of this world frighten you, you cannot fully embrace God's love as your protector. If you fear the things of this world, He will reveal those fears to you and allow you to walk through those valleys in life as the fear manifests itself. Rest assured, God will watch over you. God's preference is for you to be proactive and to overcome your fear through His Word and place your trust in Him so that He can lead you down the right path.

But the eyes of the LORD are on those who fear him,
on those whose hope is in his unfailing love. ³

The Lord watches over those who fear and revere Him. He will be patient with you if you choose to delay your destiny. He will keep a protective eye over you. He will nudge you toward what He knows is the path that will ultimately lead you toward fulfilling His will. He is not pushy. In His grace and mercy, He will wait throughout your lifetime if He needs to. By being proactive, you're setting yourself up to move forward willingly and to be a part of the action. The alternative is to be reactive when life circumstances come your way. Make the right choice.

At some point, everyone needs a wake-up call. Sometimes that wake-up call comes in the form of a life circumstance that gets your attention. No one likes a wake-up call, but everyone knows they are necessary to move forward when you are stuck. Usually, the wake-up call arrives at a time when you feel the least prepared. Pray for understanding. God's timing is different from our timing. He will provide a solution. Cry out for God's mercy. He will give you another chance. Don't forget those moments. They are defining moments. Choose to redeem the second chances that God gives you to stop delaying your destiny.

I will both lie down in peace, and sleep;
For You alone, O LORD, make me dwell in safety. [4]

The safest place you can be is in the presence of God. The safest place you can reside is the shelter of His wings. Your safe haven here on earth is in an environment where you can surround yourself with God's people, who seek to draw the presence of God. He promises throughout His Word time and time again that He will keep you safe. Though we sometimes can't understand how He is working in situations that don't feel safe, remember that He cannot lie.

"Wherever your treasure is, there the desires of your heart will also be." [5]

Whose will are you pursuing? Studying your behavioral patterns tells you everything you need to know about your priorities and whose will you are pursuing. Documenting one week of your activities will help you identify if your desires for carrying out God's will match your activities. His desires need to supersede your own agenda.

Distractions, obsessions, and preoccupations are the enemy of focusing on God's will. Anything that commands your attention and consumes your physical, mental, and emotional energy—leaving you exhausted and unable to carry out God's will or to be obedient to His Word—is unhealthy. If you are unclear about your distractions, obsessions, and preoccupations, ask your loved ones. I assure you they will quickly point out your time-consuming activities, hopefully in love and grace! Once you've acknowledged and identified your distractions, obsessions, and preoccupations, you can consider replacing those activities with behavioral patterns and actions that would further your mission to carry out God's will. It will require a change of priority. God's will must take precedence to your own will. His priorities, desires, and vision will become yours. His mission will become your mission. **Your heart ... will become His heart.**

Mission Principle 11
Let go. Stop wasting time on unhealthy obsessions.

Day 11

Path to Progress

Desire for God to revive your soul. *Psalm 19:7*
Choose not to waver in following God and to stay on His path.
Psalm 17:5
Decide God's promises are pure. *Psalm 12:6*
The **result** is the Lord watches over you if you fear Him. *Psalm 33:18*
The **promise** is the Lord will keep you safe. *Psalm 4:8*

Question from Jesus
"Can any one of you by worrying add a single hour to your life?" [6]

Questions to Meditate On
Have you shared your biggest worries openly with God in prayer?
What cares of this world are delaying your destiny?
What eternal value do those cares hold?
What unhealthy distractions can you let go of?

Your Call to Action
Embrace your future. Give up unhealthy obsessions.
Move forward. Stop delaying your destiny.

PRIORITIZE YOUR LIFE

Why is it that Christians struggle to follow Jesus's example? In today's day and age, most Christians try to convert non-believers with a salvation prayer and then disciple them. Christ did it the other way around. When Christ was on this earth, He led by example. He called His disciples to follow Him before they believed He was the Messiah. They came to believe as they walked with Him. Right before Jesus went home and ascended to heaven, He gave His disciples an irrefutable final command: *"Go and **make disciples** of all nations, baptizing them in the name of the Father and of the Son and of the Holy Spirit."* [1]

Nearly every Bible-believing Christian I know is aware of this Scripture. Yet, besides pastors and ministry leaders, only a small percentage of Bible-believing Christians actually obey this command on a daily basis. Why? The simple answer is disobedience. Intentional or not, the bottom line is discipleship is a low priority in most Christians' agendas.

Today, a cultural Christian's priorities might look something like this:

1. Attend church or live stream on Sunday on a *weekly* basis.
2. Fellowship with like-minded believers and church members on a *daily* basis.
3. Volunteer at church or at a local non-profit ministry on a *sporadic* basis.
4. Read the Bible over and over again on a *sporadic* basis.
5. Disciple someone if asked and if no one else is available on a *sporadic* basis.

If you submit to a kingdom lifestyle with Christ-like priorities, your spiritual agenda becomes:

1. Carry out God's will for your life on a **daily** basis.
2. Develop your godly character on a **daily** basis.
3. Disciple new believers with God's Word on a **daily** basis.
4. Attend church on Sunday in person to praise God and focus on Him on a **weekly** basis.
5. Fellowship and volunteer with like-minded believers and church members as time allows.

Jesus sheds light on how He feels you should prioritize His will in your life. *"Anyone who loves their father or mother more than me is not worthy of me; anyone who loves their son or daughter more than me is not worthy of me."* [2]

Are you busy being busy? There is no time like the present to make a change. Imagine God gives you a call or sends you a text one day and this is your response: "Can I call you back? I'm busy. I'm sorry, God, but my schedule is really full right now." The obligations and cares for the things in this world will choke your fruitfulness. Jesus explained in the parable of the sower what happens when the cares of this world overshadow the desire to place God's will and His kingdom above your own worldly desires.

"A farmer went out to sow his seed. As he was scattering the seed, some fell along the path, and the birds came and ate it up. Some fell on rocky places, where it did not have much soil. It sprang up quickly, because the soil was shallow. But when the sun came up, the plants were scorched, and they withered because they had no root. ***Other seed fell among thorns, which grew up and choked the plants.*** *Still other seed fell on good soil, where it produced a crop—a hundred, sixty or thirty times what was sown."* [3]

Jesus then explained the parable of the sower to His disciples:

"Listen then to what the parable of the sower means: When anyone hears the message about the kingdom and does not understand it, the evil one comes and snatches away what was sown in their heart. This is the seed sown along the path. The seed falling on

*rocky ground refers to someone who hears the word and at once receives it with joy. But since they have no root, they last only a short time. When trouble or persecution comes because of the word, they quickly fall away. **The seed falling among the thorns refers to someone who hears the word, but the worries of this life and the deceitfulness of wealth choke the word, making it unfruitful.** But the seed falling on good soil refers to someone who hears the word and understands it. This is the one who produces a crop, yielding a hundred, sixty or thirty times what was sown." [4]*

Time and time again, the Bible explains the fleeting nature and worthlessness of worldly desires compared to the eternal treasures waiting for those who carry out God's will. *The world and its desires will pass away, but **whoever does the will of God** lives forever. [5] "What good will it be for someone to gain the whole world, yet forfeit their soul?"* [6]

Commit your way to the LORD,
Trust also in Him,
And He shall bring it to pass.
He shall bring forth your righteousness as the light,
And your justice as the noonday. [7]

Do it all for the Lord. Prioritize your life so that everything that you do is centered around Him. You are no longer doing things out of self-gratification, achievement, or approval of others but rather to serve the One who has called you to the work of serving others. As long as your activities and goals are ultimately geared toward sharing the gospel, discipling others, and developing your godly character, you can rest assured that you are within God's will. Commit everything that you do unto the Lord by following His instructions.

Who, then, are those who fear the LORD?
He will instruct them in the ways they should choose.
They will spend their days in prosperity,
and their descendants will inherit the land. [8]

When you set up your weekly calendar, align it with a kingdom schedule so that you may carry out God's will first and foremost every single day. From your first breath in the morning, put your best energy into carrying out God's will. Your energy tends to fade as the day goes on, so give Him your freshest energy.

"You are worthy, our Lord and God,
to receive glory and honor and power,
for you created all things,
and by your will they were created
and have their being." [9]

Jesus is to be treasured. He deserves to be the highest priority in your schedule. It's easy to get caught up in the day-to-day tasks and be consumed by your worldly passions. Interests can quickly evolve into obsessions that will keep you fully distracted. These obsessions may evolve into idols in your life. Only when you focus your attention on Jesus can you give Him the love and devotion that He deserves. When you place idols in place of your love for Jesus, you hinder the Holy Spirit's ability to help direct your life. Remove the idols and distractions in your life today. "How do I identify them?" you ask. Document your daily routines and review your bank statement. Your idols will be staring you right in the face.

Mission Principle 12
Get your priorities straight. Love God above all else.

Path to Progress

Desire to keep the ways of God. *Psalm 18:21*
Choose to love the Lord your God. *Psalm 18:1*
Decide to commit all your actions to God. *Psalm 37:5*
The **result** is, if you fear the Lord, you will be shown the path you should choose, which leads to prosperity, and your children will inherit the land. *Psalm 25:12-13*
The **promise** is the Lord will reward you for doing the right thing.
Psalm 18:20

Question from Jesus
"What good will it be for someone to gain the whole world, yet forfeit their soul?" [10]

Questions to Meditate On
What takes precedence in your life?
What impact does your *busyness* have on eternal matters?
What person or thing consumes the majority of your attention?
Do you wholeheartedly put God *above* all else?

Your Call to Action
Start discipling. Stop idolizing.
Put God first. Prioritize your life.

MISSION FINDER STORY
51/50 FOR JESUS

Many poor people realize their need for Jesus. I've encountered many homeless on the street who are sold out for Jesus. They are more clear about their faith, and doing God's will, than many well-to-do Christians who have crossed my path. My homeless friend Supernatural Sage radiates Jesus on every corner he stands on in La Jolla, California. His name alone should tell you that his story is unique. La Jolla is renowned as a world-class destination, known for its wealth, yet it has a significant and growing homeless population. It's become a visible, real world illustration of the wealth gap in America.

My friend Sage knows how to *bear much fruit*. Every day, he stands on one of the busiest intersection islands in La Jolla evangelizing to the cars driving by, and to people walking by, showing his signs with words of encouragement and Bible verses. Meanwhile, some of the wealthiest individuals in Southern California line up, in their six- and seven-figure cars, at one of the longest red lights in San Diego to take in this amazing sight every morning and afternoon.

Sage often walks down the island of the intersection holding a yellow tennis ball with a smiley face etched on it with a permanent marker. Holding up the tennis ball and shaking it, he will then say: "Smile for Jesus." The reaction he gets from the people sitting in their cars waiting for the light to turn green is priceless. He frequently hands out T-shirts that he creates for some of San Diego's wealthiest residents that read *Power Princess for Jesus* for the ladies and *Warrior for Christ* for the men. He often wears his favorite T-shirt, which says *Jesus Loves You*. The evangelism of this homeless man to the unsaved local citizens and visitors of La Jolla has a profound impact on people in a most unexpected location.

When the police would threaten to arrest him, he would reply with one of my favorite expressions of all time:

"Forgive me, Officer, I'm 51/50 [crazy] for Jesus."

The joy of the Lord overflows from this man's heart. At first glance, you might think this man really is crazy. What possible impact could he have? Let me tell you from firsthand experience: the impact is profound. He is stone cold sober. No drugs, no alcohol, no mental illness, nor any other stigma that is usually attached to the homeless. Sage is the real deal. A street evangelist at heart who decided twenty years ago that living outdoors was preferable to his lifestyle and mission than living indoors. By the world's standard and in terms of worldly currency, he is poor. By the kingdom's standards and in terms of heavenly currency, this man is wealthy. I look forward to visiting his mansion in heaven.

Part I

SUMMARY: HOW TO FIND GOD'S WILL

Your will is what determines your path in life. You discover *Jesus's will* was to love His Father, which embodied obedience and fulfilling His Father's will. You learn *God's will* is for you to love Him above all else, bring the kingdom of heaven to earth, bear fruit in your life, make disciples, seek Him with all your heart, and pray to Him. God promises to provide you a future and a hope. After comparing your will to Jesus's will to God's will, you have a better understanding of God's will for your life.

Just like Jesus, you are "about your *Father's business.*" Your eyes are opened to the *big picture.* You believe that God sees something special in you and desires to reveal it to you. By *shaping your vision,* you are able to clearly *spot the roadblocks ahead.* You learn how to *break the chains* in your life through God's promises in His Word. You endeavor to *follow Jesus* and obey His instructions. You obey God's commandments and *accept mission possible.* You overcome your doubts and fears. You *stop delaying your destiny.* You *prioritize your life* to reflect kingdom activities that honor the Lord and display your obedience to His Word. You are inspired to pursue God's will based on God's promises.

You start to apply the information you learn through the *Path to Progress* section at the end of each chapter. You start to question what God's will for your life is. You are prayerful to ask the Holy Spirit to help you find God's will for your life. You find God's will by expressing a desire, then making good choices that lead to wise decisions. You commit to pursuing your calling. You are ready to grasp the knowledge, understanding, and wisdom that will be required to fulfill God's will. You are ready to move forward.

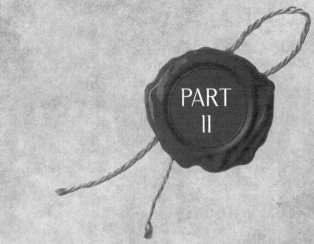

PART
II

FULFILL GOD'S WILL FOR YOUR LIFE

INTRODUCTION

Your mission is to bear fruit for God. In order to fulfill God's will and complete your mission to produce a harvest, you will need divine knowledge, understanding, and wisdom, all found in the Bible. To *bear fruit*, you will need to obey God's instructions, disciple others, and reveal your heart's true intentions.

Authentic Intentions

God has now revealed to us his mysterious will regarding Christ—which is to fulfill his own good plan. [1]

Your intention determines your destination. Start off on the right foot by studying divine knowledge inside the Bible. No matter which mission-driven kingdom assignment you choose, it will require you to reveal the treasure of your heart and expand your human understanding. Throughout your calling, you will be faced with choices and decisions. You will be presented with obstacles to overcome. God's wisdom will provide you the solutions to overcome these obstacles.

Authentic Instructions

To fulfill God's will for your life, you need to understand the instructions and words of Jesus. What exactly has Jesus commanded you to do? Jesus gave you two primary commandments. *"'Love the Lord your God with all your heart and with all your soul and with all your mind.' This is the first and greatest commandment. And the second is like it: 'Love your neighbor as yourself.'"* [2]

Authentic Obedience

Jesus is interested in an eternal relationship with you. He seeks a close and deepening relationship with you. *"As the Father loved Me, I also have loved you; abide in My love. If you keep My commandments, you will abide in My love, just as I have kept My Father's commandments and abide in His love."* [3] *Jesus said to the people who believed in him, "You are truly my disciples if you remain faithful to my teachings. And you will know the truth, and the truth will set you free."* [4]

Authentic Discipleship

Authentic discipleship is teaching one another about God's Word. By learning about His ways and His character, we learn how to carry out His will by obeying His commands. Developing Christ-like character is the result of discipleship. Discipleship is all about being vulnerable. It requires trust in the guidance of a mature brother or sister in Christ. It's a season to look deep within yourself and overcome being satisfied with the status quo. *"Teach these new disciples to obey all the commands I have given you. And be sure of this: I am with you always, even to the end of the age."* [5]

Find the right person to disciple you. The world is full of mentors and coaches, but it lacks disciplers and disciple makers. Why is that? The short answer is disobedience mixed with various excuses. The long answer is that today's culture pays little respect to Christ's commands. The world has replaced discipleship with mentoring and coaching for a variety of worldly interests. We now find ourselves in a place where developing or learning skills for worldly purposes takes priority over developing or learning discipleship skills to bring the kingdom of heaven here on earth. *"My command is this: Love each other as I have loved you."* [6]

What is the difference between a coach, a mentor, a discipler, and a disciple maker? This is not a trick question. A simple definition is this:

A *mentor* teaches you a skill that you do not possess. A *coach* keeps you accountable to grow a skill you already possess. A *discipler* teaches you the Word of God to help you develop your spiritual character. A *disciple maker* teaches you how to impart spiritual character into another disciple and teaches you how to create more disciples. The results are multiplication.

Why is this so important? Without becoming a disciple maker, you cannot carry out God's will of discipleship to its full potential. Do not settle into the world's system of mentorship or coaching. If Jesus wanted us to coach or mentor others, He would've done it Himself. He chose to disciple others and taught us to make disciples. Discipleship is part of God's will for every believer. *"By this everyone will know that you are my disciples, if you love one another."* [7]

As you embark on Part Two of the *Mission Finder* journey, you will focus on four application steps to help you fulfill God's will.

- Step 4 is to *study the Bible*, God's blueprint of divine knowledge.
- Step 5 is to *cleanse your heart and mind* by revealing what you treasure.
- Step 6 is to *choose the right path* using God's wisdom.
- Step 7 is to *carry out your mission* by never giving up.

Let's get underway with Part Two, as we learn how to *fulfill* God's will for your life and move you toward hearing those precious words we all long for … "Well done, good and faithful servant."

step four

STUDY THE BIBLE

KNOWLEDGE

IGNITE YOUR DESIRE FOR JUSTICE

For the LORD is righteous,
he loves justice;
the upright will see his face. [1]

Choose to love justice. Stand in the gap for those who are experiencing injustice. Desire for the injustices of this world to come to an end. It will take individuals who are willing to stand up and fulfill God's will to squash these injustices. When you ignite your desire to love the things that God cares about, which include mercy, faith, justice, and generosity, you can start to walk the walk. By studying His blueprint for justice, you can access His divine knowledge to learn how to conquer injustices in the world.

The Bible outlines many injustices in mankind's history. The stories are not there for entertainment but to learn from. The stories have details and solutions that specifically give insight on how to overcome injustice. It's within the details of those stories you are able to gain the understanding and wisdom necessary to apply the ways of those who came before you who overcame and conquered injustice.

The LORD examines the righteous,
but the wicked, those who love violence,
he hates with a passion. [2]

God hates violence. Join Him in that passion. Reject violence in your life. Don't stir the pot or encourage hateful words, but rather encourage soft, kind, and encouraging words. Violence is the result of hatred, and hatred is the result of anger. Anger is usually the result of hurtful words or actions. God is a God of peace who loves justice and teaches His followers to be virtuous.

The decision to be virtuous precedes righteous behavior. You can become a virtuous person by living an ethical life. A virtuous person is compassionate and humble and embodies the fruit of the Spirit. Their vocabulary edifies the recipient. A virtuous person has a high standard of excellence in how they conduct themselves. They communicate pleasantly, build others up frequently, and conduct themselves with integrity. By adhering to this higher standard of morals, you can develop your character to reflect Jesus Christ. Only you know in your heart what you desire. If it's to be virtuous, God will guide you through His divine knowledge on how to become a person of godly virtue. *He has shown you, O mortal, what is good. / And what does the LORD require of you? / To act justly and to love mercy / and to walk humbly with your God.* [3]

Surround yourself with good company. When you choose to love justice and hate violence and surround yourself with like-minded people, you are prepared to fulfill God's will. When you choose to distance yourself from people who are violent, hateful, and committing unrighteous acts, you create a space for God to operate and utilize your gifts and talents to further His kingdom.

Spend time in God's presence. Christians often seek the hand of God in their lives when the focus should be on the face of God. When you ignite your desire to see the face of God, you can start to look in the mirror and imagine what the reflection of His character would look like. Jesus will show you how to replicate His character traits in your life. *"He who has My commandments and keeps them, it is he who loves Me. And he who loves Me will be loved by My Father, and I will love him and manifest Myself to him."* [4]

Ignite your desire for God's Word. His commandments are a blueprint for you to become virtuous and righteous. Bible-believing Christians desire to be transformed into the image of Christ. But how exactly do you do that? A friend of mine, Don Nava, often says information plus application equals transformation. This equation can be applied to spiritual growth. Since we know that Jesus is a promise keeper, we can depend on His words as our primary source of information. By applying His instructions to our daily lives and being obedient, we can solve the application portion of the equation. The result will be doing God's will, which is the Christ-like transformation we all desire.

You, Lord, keep my lamp burning;
my God turns my darkness into light. [5]
Your word is a lamp for my feet,
a light on my path. [6]
The light shines in the darkness, and the darkness has not overcome it. [7]
"If you are filled with light, with no dark corners, then your whole life will be radiant, as though a floodlight were filling you with light." [8]

Bring glory to God by shining bright. Have you ever met somebody who seems to glow? The radiance from their smile, happiness, and joy is infectious. Where does this come from? When the Holy Spirit controls every aspect of the human spirit and darkness has no place, light infiltrates entirely. Stoke your desire to learn more about Jesus so He becomes the source of light in your life, as He is the light of the world. He will guide you to become like Him, righteous and virtuous. You will shine bright like the Morning Star. *When Jesus spoke again to the people, he said, "I am the light of the world. Whoever follows me will never walk in darkness, but will have the light of life."* [9] *"In the same way, let your light shine before others, that they may see your good deeds and glorify your Father in heaven."* [10]

Mission Principle 13
Ignite your desire to become righteous and virtuous.

Day 13

Path to Progress

Desire to see the face of God. *Psalm 11:7*
Choose to love justice and hate violence. *Psalm 11:5, 7*
Decide to be virtuous. *Psalm 11:7*
The **result** is your heart will be right. *Psalm 11:2*
The **promise** is the Lord will watch you closely, and
He observes the righteous and the wicked. *Psalm 11:4-5*

Question from Jesus
"Who is it you want?" [11]

Questions to Meditate On
What or who do you desire most in your life?
Where does that desire come from?
Are you standing in the gap of an injustice?
When you look in the mirror, do you see God's image?

Your Call to Action
Study God's words. Learn His character.
Reflect His image. Desire justice.

DISCOVER GOD'S DIVINE DESIGN

"Do to others as you would like them to do to you." [1]

God's divine design is for you to love others more than yourself. This includes being generous, developing godly character, and offering forgiveness. It also requires loving others when they aren't easy to love. These choices aren't always easy, but if you trust God, He will show you the way.

Jesus is the reassurance of God's love. God sent His son to show you His love. His desire is for all people to follow Jesus and be saved, not just the chosen few. Jesus reassures us of God's love in the Gospels through the following teachings. An expansive list is in Appendix 1.

+ You are valuable to God. [2]
+ God will care for you. [3]
+ God's will is that all who see His son and believe in Him should have eternal life. [4]
+ Jesus desires you to be with Him. [5]
+ Jesus loves you like the Father loves Him. [6]
+ Jesus will reveal Himself to those who love Him. [7]
+ Anyone who believes in Jesus will not perish but have eternal life. [8]
+ Jesus came to serve, not to be served. [9]
+ Jesus came to give His life as a ransom for many. [10]
+ Jesus gave Himself as a holy sacrifice for you so you can be made holy by God's truth. [11]
+ The greatest love is to lay down your life for your friends. [12]
+ Our love for each other will prove to the world we are Jesus's disciples. [13]

God calls His followers to display a supernatural love. You are called to love everyone who you come in contact with. You are called to do good to those who hate you, pray for those who persecute you, love your enemies, and bless those who curse you; if someone takes something from you, you are instructed not to try to get it back. [14] To operate in this manner in the world you live in today takes heavenly love and adherence to a kingdom lifestyle. Christ demonstrated for you what this looks like when He was here on earth.

Jesus is a model example of how to love others. Jesus referenced how to love others throughout the Scriptures with direct instructions on how to treat others with kindness and love regardless of the circumstance.

- Love each other. [15]
- Love those who are opposed to you. [16]
- Give to everyone who asks you. [17]
- Pray for those who mistreat you. [18]
- Do good for people who hate you. [19]
- Bless the people who curse you. [20]
- Do not only love those who love you. [21]
- If you are slapped on one cheek, let them also slap the other cheek. [22]
- If someone asks you for your coat, give them your shirt also. [23]
- Do not only lend to those who can repay you. [24]
- Be like the Good Samaritan and show your neighbor mercy. [25]

Loving others can be challenging. Loving those close to you comes naturally because they usually reciprocate your love. You may feel that those who reject, offend, persecute, antagonize, or ridicule you do not deserve your love, yet you are commanded to love those people too. *"A second [commandment] is equally important: 'Love your neighbor as yourself.'"* [26]

The way that you love your neighbor as yourself is by developing godly character. This should be the second priority in your life, after loving God, which is your primary priority. Developing godly character allows you to love others as Christ loves you. The word *neighbor* should encompass everyone who you come in contact with on a daily basis. What you will find when you display godly character is that you start to become a magnet for individuals who share a desire to pursue godly character.

Develop a godly character. You attract those who you are trying to become. You also attract those who are trying to become like you. In summary, to attract people into your life who have a wholesome character, you yourself must draw the line and decide it's time to start developing a godly character within yourself on a daily basis. How do you do that? It starts with the fruit of the Spirit. In Dr. David Jeremiah's book, *A Life Beyond Amazing,* he illustrates the fruit of the Spirit and all the attributes of a godly character. [27] These attributes are the key to loving like Christ. *But the fruit of the Spirit is love, joy, peace, forbearance, kindness, goodness, faithfulness, gentleness and self-control. Against such things there is no law.* [28]

Mission Principle 14
Love others more than yourself. No excuses.

PATH TO PROGRESS

Desire to love one another, since love comes from God. *1 John 4:7*
Choose to rely on God's love. *1 John 4:16*
Decide God's unfailing love for you will not be shaken. *Isaiah 54:10*
The **result** is if you live in love, you live in God, and God lives in you.
1 John 4:16
The **promise** is that if you do not love, you do not know God
because God is love. *1 John 4:8*

Question from Jesus
"If you love those who love you, what reward will you get?" [29]

Questions to Meditate On
Are you loving others more than yourself?
Is your focus on serving others or serving yourself?
Are you placing strangers' needs before your own needs?
Do you believe God loves you?

Your Call to Action
Focus on others. Help others in need.
Love others. Discover the divine design.

Day 15

FILTER OUT THE NOISE IN YOUR LIFE

Keep a close watch on how you live and on your teaching. Stay
true to what is right for the sake of your own salvation and
the salvation of those who hear you. [1]

Listen for God's voice to hear God's will. Learn how to filter the noise
out of your life. Learn how to ignore the distractions and concerns of
your day. Learn to protect your mind from all negative elements coming
at you. This will be essential to stay on the right path to fulfill God's will.

What makes your life noisy? Any inbound information that creates fear,
anxiety, or worry that doesn't allow you to be fully focused and present
with God needs to cease. It produces nothing that is beneficial for your
long-term well-being. Your time on earth is limited. God's plan for your
life is waiting to be fulfilled. Every moment you focus on the noise in
your life is a precious moment lost that could have been spent doing the
will of God.

God will keep you on this planet as long as He needs you here. Once
you give your life to Him, you can rest assured that you have an eternal
destination. Never forget where your true security resides. You actually
have no risk once you've submitted your life wholly to God. You start
to realize in the event that you need to go home to heaven earlier than
you hoped, you're going to be in a better place than you are right now.
So what is there to worry about? What is there to be concerned about?
Why is fear even on your radar screen? You should sleep soundly at
night unless you don't truly believe in God's protection or you do not really desire to have peace in your life. This means there is still something

inside your mind that is hindering peace. Some form of insecurity or distrust that is not allowing you to fully trust in Him. This usually comes from noise in your life. Analyze the noise in your life to figure out what is robbing you of resting in His peace, abiding in His protection. *The LORD is my shepherd, I lack nothing. / He makes me lie down in green pastures, / he leads me beside quiet waters, / he refreshes my soul. / He guides me along the right paths / for his name's sake.* [2]

When you lie down, you will not be afraid;
Yes, you will lie down and your sleep will be sweet. [3]

There's nothing like a great night's sleep. Insomnia can drive you to the brink of insanity. Fear, anxiety, and concern are typically the main causes that inhibit sound sleep. If you want your soul to be refreshed, cleansed of fear, worry, and anxiety, spend time in Proverbs and dive into the wisdom and knowledge that God offers.

"Those who listen to my [Jesus's] message and believe in God ... have eternal life." [4]

Listen to Jesus. Just because you can hear someone or something doesn't mean you're actively or intently listening. Listening takes focus, intent, and no distractions. Listening requires the recipient to clear their mind and be fully present to the message at hand. When you listen to God's message with an intent to do it, transformation occurs in your heart. When sharing the Word of God with others, listen to their heart. Listen for the clues, listen for God speaking to you and through you.

So then faith comes by hearing, and hearing by the word of God. [5]

Are you fully present? My wife reminds me quite often that I am hard of hearing. However, it seems to me that my hearing is perfectly fine. There somehow seems to be a disconnect between me being fully present and listening intently versus selectively hearing what I want to hear. The natural inclination is to only allow my mind to think about the things I desire to think about, while pretending to intently listen to others. I find the same to be true when it comes to sharing my faith with others who do not believe in Christ. There's a lot of selective hearing that goes on when that conversation kicks off. Often times, the moment I bring up the words God or faith, the person's eyes and mind drift elsewhere and I find they're not one hundred percent present.

Is something preventing you from clearly listening to God's message?
Life circumstances can weigh down your heart and paralyze your steps forward to carry out God's will. Remember that God promises your mourning will not be in vain. Healing comes through teardrops. God is your comforter, and through your journey, He will set up situations for your healing to take place. But you need to move forward. You cannot stay frozen. You have to unthaw. *"Blessed are those who mourn, for they will be comforted."* [6]

Regardless of whatever adversity, tragedy, or life circumstance has come your way, understand that once you commit to fulfill God's will for your life, mental, physical, emotional, and spiritual healing can begin to take place. While you are frozen, your enemy Satan can have his way by persecuting, debilitating, and discouraging you so that ultimately you feel defeated. Although it may feel real, this is an illusion. Satan cannot defeat you if you are saved by Christ. Jesus already won the battle on Calvary. Satan can, however, encourage you to take the wrong path, make the wrong decisions, and try to convince you that you are incapable of fulfilling God's will.

To defeat Satan, filter the noise by staying focused on your biblical beliefs. My family lays out a yearly calendar to focus on core values and biblical beliefs every single month. Our beliefs are what trigger our behavior. Therefore, we need to adhere to our beliefs so we can carry out the core values in our lives. For example, in the month of January, our biblical belief is that God is real and our core value is encouragement. Believing that God is real, alive, and cares about us inspires us to encourage one another and the others in our lives. The biblical beliefs and core values go hand in hand. The beliefs feed the values, and the values feed the behavior.

Here are a few steps to get you started if you wish to document your biblical beliefs and core values for yourself or your family. First, decide what you value. Second, believe that change within yourself or your family is possible. Third, demonstrate that you believe in the value enough to display that behavior on a daily basis.

I created an illustration of my family's core values, biblical beliefs, and priorities for us to follow. I print mine regularly and distribute it to all members of my immediate and extended family. It can be found in several places in my household. You will find it on the wall, on the dining table during holiday gatherings, and inside everyone's bedside table. It keeps the family members focused on God's will and all on the same page. I design a similar illustration for any company I am appointed to steward.

Mission Principle 15
Remove distractions to hear clear
communication from God.

ARROYO FAMILY
VISION, MISSION, BELIEFS, & LIFE PURPOSE STATEMENT

PURPOSE: **OBEY GOD'S WORD**
VISION: **BEAR MUCH FRUIT**
MISSION: **DO GOD'S WILL**

BIBLICAL BELIEFS:
January: **God Is Real**
February: **Discipleship**
March: **Holy Spirit Lifestyle**
April: **Love Never Fails**
May: **Obedience**
June: **No Fear**
July: **Wisdom Is Priceless**
August: **The Great Commission**
September: **Our Burden Is Light**
October: **No Doubt**
November: **Praise & Worship**
December: **Christ Is King**

PRIORITIES:
Carry out God's will for our life
Develop godly character
Strengthen marriage
Disciple family
Fellowship
with friends
Focus on
self

ARROYO FAMILY
CORE VALUES:

January: **Encouragement**

February: **Physical Touch**

March: **Communication**

April: **Joy**

May: **Kindness**

June: **Generosity**

July: **Quality Time**

August: **Love**

September: **Affirmations**

October: **Compassion**

November: **Forgiveness**

December: **Gifts**

Path to Progress

Desire to sleep soundly without fear. *Proverbs 3:24*
Choose not to lose sight of common sense and discernment. Hang tight
to them. *Proverbs 3:21*
Decide that the Lord is your security. *Proverbs 3:26*
The **result** is common sense and discernment will refresh your soul.
Proverbs 3:22
The **promise** is knowledge will create joy in your life. *Proverbs 2:10*

Question from Jesus
"Why is my language not clear to you?" [7]

Questions to Meditate On
What is the noise in your life you need to get rid of?
What distractions prevent you from reading God's Word?
Is the daily information filling your mind healthy?
How can you filter the flow of negative information?

Your Call to Action
Seek the truth. Read the Word.
Let go of distractions. Filter out the noise.

Day 16

ACCEPT GOD'S PROMISES

The words of the LORD are pure words,
Like silver tried in a furnace of earth,
Purified seven times. [1]

God promises that His promises are pure. When you accept God's promises as pure truth, you will be able to focus on the letters and details of His promises. If you are skeptical about His promises, you will spend the majority of your time analyzing whether or not the promises are true. If you have been subject to broken promises in your life, it can be initially challenging to accept God's promises, especially when others in your life have broken their word.

This world is full of promise makers and promise breakers, but the world's way is not God's way. The world's way is to make promises, then break promises, then change the truth, reword the promises, and justify those broken promises with more lies. God cannot lie. He began as holy and will remain holy. *Jesus Christ is the same yesterday, today, and forever.* [2] So are the promises He has made.

You are not alone. God's promises are meant to give you security, provide you shelter, and solidify your trust in His sovereignty. However, it's up to you to accept His promises and to apply His promises in your life. Your own doubt and unbelief can get in the way. Look at God's promises in the Bible and note which ones have already come true in your life; this will serve as a great reminder that God is faithful. He shows Himself faithful to us so that we can, in turn, be faithful to Him.

Decide, once and for all, that God's Word is the way, the truth, and the life. This way you can start to explore how to utilize His promises in your everyday life. Your trust in Him grows by opening your heart and mind to the fact that His promises will never waver. Your trust in Him deepens as what you once held to be true fades. This is the journey that every person walking the straight and narrow path is experiencing. *My son, keep my words, / And treasure my commands within you.* [3]

God's love for you is illustrated through His son, Jesus. After you have accepted God's promises, the next step is to treasure His son. God's promises, through Jesus, are in essence another form of His love for you. His promises are designed to directly impact your life. This is what God proclaimed through His son, Jesus:

+ We are united with God through the name of Jesus. [4]
+ The names of God and Jesus are powerful and protect us. [5]
+ The Father sent His son to earth to save it, not to judge it. [6]
+ You find eternal life by knowing the one true God and Jesus, whom He sent. [7]

Meditate on the intention behind God's promises. Seek out the meaning of His promises and don't take them for granted. Learn to understand what's behind His promises. Read them again and again. What you will discover is that when you treasure His son and His commands, you come into alignment with God. His promises were all designed out of His abundant love for you and specifically for your well-being.

+ God's Word is the truth. [8]
+ Anything is possible with God. [9]
+ Jesus is the bread of life that came down from heaven. Anyone who eats the bread of heaven will live forever and never die. [10]
+ God knows exactly what you need even before you ask. [11]

Allow God's promises to reside in your heart. In order to store God's promises deep within your heart and to call upon them, there has to be a desire for those promises to be written on your heart. Start today by taking time to meditate on a handful of His promises. *"I take joy in doing* *your will, my God, for your instructions are written on my heart."* [12] To help you get started, here is a list to choose from. A comprehensive list can be found in Appendix 1. Discover more on your own by opening God's treasure chest of promises, the Bible.

+ God is more powerful than anyone else. [13]
+ God and Jesus are one. [14]
+ God gave Jesus authority over everyone. [15]
+ Jesus is the Alpha and Omega, the First and Last, the Beginning and the End. [16]
+ Jesus's words won't ever disappear, even after heaven and earth are gone. [17]
+ There will be multiple false prophets, and many people will believe their deceptions. [18]
+ Jesus will raise up His followers on the last day. [19]
+ It is foolish to be rich in earthly things but not in your relationship with God. [20]
+ You need to be more righteous than the teachers of the law and Pharisees to enter the kingdom of heaven. [21]

This next step of the journey is to cleanse your heart and mind. Now that you better understand how to study God's Word, the next step is to use wisdom and understanding to discover the treasures in His Word.

Mission Principle 16
Accept God's promises.
They are designed for your well-being.

Path to Progress

Desire God's instructions to be written on your heart. *Psalm 40:8*
Choose to always treasure God's commands. *Proverbs 7:1*
Decide that God's way is perfect and the Lord's promises are true.
Psalm 18:30
The **result** is you will receive the Lord's blessing and have a righteous
relationship with God your savior. *Psalm 24:5*
The **promise** is you are fool if you say in your heart that there
isn't a God. *Psalm 14:1*

Question from Jesus
"If I am telling the truth, why don't you believe me?" [22]

Questions to Meditate On
Do any of God's promises create doubt in your mind?
Which promises stand out and are most applicable in your life?
Is your mission based on one or more of God's promises?
What agreements have you made with yourself or others that contradict
God's promises?

Your Call to Action
Explore God's Word. Receive God's love.
Discover God's plan. Accept God's promises.

MISSION FINDER STORY
THROUGH THE EYE OF A NEEDLE

Then Jesus said to His disciples, "Assuredly, I say to you that it is hard for a rich man to enter the kingdom of heaven. And again I say to you, it is easier for a camel to go through the eye of a needle than for a rich man to enter the kingdom of God." [1]

People often ask me, "How did you make it?" What they are really asking is *how did I succeed in the business world.* I share with them the steps that brought me worldly success in my book *7 Steps to a Paycheck,* but I emphasize the real success in my journey began when I opened my heart and mind to God's will for my life. I also share the deceitfulness of riches and the story in the Gospel of Matthew of the young, rich ruler who Jesus discussed in the Bible verse above. I was so moved by this verse when I first read it that it quickly became a theme in my life and ultimately inspired me to want to give away as much of my wealth as possible.

The most important life-changing decision a person will ever make is that of personal faith: to believe or not to believe, what to believe, and how to carry out those beliefs. Once I was clear on my beliefs and God's will for my life, I started a charitable organization named Eye of a Needle Foundation to fulfill His will. It was primarily funded by the charitable donations of my real estate company, AARE. Twenty percent of our company's profit on every transaction goes to charities like Eye of a Needle. I believe that with abundant resources comes the responsibility to help those in need.

The agents, brokers, and employees stand behind the company's goals and mission. Together we believe in the direction we're moving in because there is a clearly defined cause that motivates us as a company, which is to serve and bless others. We're careful to protect the company's culture by inviting agents who have shown themselves to be honest, ethical, good-hearted, cooperative, hard-working, and of a giving and sharing nature. As the founder, I have great appreciation for every agent and staff member. Their giving, sharing, caring, and ethical dealings make me proud to be their leader, while their hard work enables us to reach out charitably to our community and to the world.

Over the years, we have stayed true to the biblical principles the company was founded upon. We started out by partnering with secular and faith-based programs worldwide in an effort to support various humanitarian and social improvement projects. The initial projects included: homeless services, shelter for orphans, prison ministry, outreach to communities of extreme poverty, rescuing street children, providing medicine where health care is scarce, and supporting missionaries.

Natural beauty is helping others. In 2012, our mission expanded when Eye of a Needle Foundation acquired Missionfinder.org. The Mission Finder website features one of the largest directories worldwide of mission organizations that volunteers and donors can access to serve and support. The website also provides a comprehensive online community for users to search mission opportunities around the world. Through the use of this technology, the foundation was able to dramatically increase the number of organizations and individuals it was supporting.

Although the charity was moving in the right direction, I still felt an internal struggle. Was I supposed to slow down with real estate and focus on the charity? Was God's will for my life in ministry or in real estate? How could I balance building the charity while still growing the income of the real estate company? Was it possible to do both?

What God revealed to me is that when you put His will above your self-interest, He will give you the vision to move forward. You can choose any vocation and still carry out His will. You don't need to leave your job, become part of the pastoral staff at your local church, or turn into a lifetime missionary to carry out His will. Anyone can be utilized to effectively carry out His purposes in any setting. He also revealed a way for me to give more to charity while turning the real estate company into a workplace ministry.

Your intentions determine your inventions. This phrase came to me as I was developing a new program to increase the charitable giving at AARE. You know you have been called to do something when passion overcomes you. You are no longer working or "doing your job," but rather you are fulfilling your purpose. As I mentioned, my real estate company has a passion for charity and has made a commitment to give back generously. With that in mind, we developed a unique program called Generous Giving aimed at giving financial assistance to nonprofit organizations, churches, ministries, and missions. Real estate agents, homeowners, donors, and business owners can all participate in the program. Here is how it works ...

Someone refers us a client who buys, sells, or leases a business, residential, or commercial property anywhere in the United States. When the real estate transaction is completed, AARE gives back a significant portion of the commission to a charitable organization. Depending on the final sales price, AARE donates ten to forty percent of the total commission directly to the client's charity of choice. This donation program is in addition to the twenty percent in charitable contributions the company currently donates from its gross profits. For example, assume a real estate agent represents a new client in a real estate transaction for $1 million, and the company earns a three percent commission of the purchase or selling price. This would yield a gross commission of $30,000. Thirty percent of the gross commission is given to charity, which in this case is $9,000.

This *invention* allowed me to fulfill God's will as He shaped and directed my *intention* of blessing others. What started this program was an understanding that donors are always looking for creative ways to give more to the charities they love and support. It takes a lot of hard work and dedication for nonprofit charities to produce significant recurring donations. Through my research, I discovered that more than five million properties are sold annually in the United States. These transactions generate an estimated $70 billion dollars in real-estate commissions every year. This has allowed our company to generate significant contributions for the charities our clients love and support on an ongoing basis without donors having to write more checks. My hope and prayer is that other CEOs and founders inspired by this idea will model this unique and creative giving approach and turn their companies into workplace ministries.

We're excited to be expanding our reach to help more organizations keep their vision and mission alive. The successful sale or acquisition of one property can change the life of a homeless family or help translate Bible verses into languages across the globe. God has taught me to look for a significant return on my investments, not only in monetary gains but, more importantly, in human terms. Developing the Generous Giving program taught me that when pursuing God's will, anything is possible.

When His disciples heard it, they were greatly astonished, saying, "Who then can be saved?"
But Jesus looked at them and said to them, "With men this is impossible, but with God all things are possible." [2]

step five

CLEANSE YOUR HEART & MIND

UNDERSTANDING

IDENTIFY YOUR HEART'S TREASURE

"It is written, 'Man shall not live by bread alone, but by every word that proceeds from the mouth of God.'"[1]

Your heart is like a treasure chest. You can fill it up with all sorts of things, including the desires of this world, painful memories of the past, or any number of worldly idols, in an attempt to feel fulfilled. Our hearts tend to have an insatiable need to chase the next best thing. These temporal fixes or "must-have" fads many times lead to a heavy and numb heart or disappointment. Each day, choose to fill up with the truth, which is the Word of God. It will enrich you and jumpstart your heart every morning into the right rhythm.

Renew your heart with God's truths. This is the way God intended for you to live from the beginning of time. Christ reminded us that man and woman should not eat only bread. Man and woman should have a daily hunger and thirst for the Word of God. Experience the richness and taste of God's Word. Knowing the absolute truth allows you to block evil thoughts, antagonistic people, worldly desires, the lust of the eye, comfort for the body, and fleeting desires that you know in your heart of hearts will pass away in time.

"Your eye is the lamp of your body. When your eyes are healthy, your whole body also is full of light. But when they are unhealthy, your body also is full of darkness. See to it, then, that the light within you is not darkness."[2]

Words and images impact your mind and shape your heart. What you allow into your heart and mind directly affects your well-being. Worldly inputs that you absorb on a regular basis will determine what you contribute back into the world. Filling your mind, heart, eyes, and ears with healthy, quality content develops godly character. Worship music, moral media viewing choices, and positive news resources will all help your heart's output.

"A good person produces good things from the treasury of a good heart, and an evil person produces evil things from the treasury of an evil heart." [3]

Evil can disguise itself to be something amazing that's going to give you ongoing satisfaction, but in the end, every time, it results in feelings of guilt, shame, and loss. It steals, kills, and destroys. Why are we so drawn to it? Why do we feel the need to engage with imagery, sounds, or physical touches that we know are not righteous? What makes it so seductive? The deception behind evil is false hope. A false truth with a magnetic draw.

"For from within, out of a person's heart, come evil thoughts, sexual immorality, theft, murder, adultery, greed, wickedness, deceit, lustful desires, envy, slander, pride, and foolishness." [4]

Can you overcome the evil in your heart? Yes. You can overcome the evil in your heart today by replacing the treasure in your heart. We all have a treasury in our hearts. Some stockpile a treasure of money, assets, and tangible items that provide temporary comfort in this life. Others stockpile a treasury of memories, photos, and videos documenting the seasons of life. Others stockpile a treasury of antiques or memorabilia, therefore living in the past. Others stockpile treasures for the future, hope for better technology, and easier functionality in an idealistic society.

We are creatures of habit who deep down desire change. Yet we lean toward complacency and are frequently averse to any substantial change. The challenge within our hearts that we all face is removing the treasures that prevent us from spiritual growth and replacing them with healthy, eternal treasures. Imagine a stockpile of gold sitting in your basement, something you've worked for slowly, accumulated at the right price: it holds tremendous value, and it gives you a sense of security. One day you discover that the gold-plated bars, your security blanket of sorts, are completely worthless poured concrete. Slowly you start to remove one gold bar at a time and replace it with a godly character trait that will last for eternity. What are your gold bars? What is in your heart's treasury? Whatever that treasure is, let it go. Replace it with something eternal, like love for God's Word.

"For whatever is in your heart determines what you say." [5]

If what's in your heart determines what you say, then make it a priority to shape and develop a heart full of goodness coupled with joy. Be someone who lifts others up. Be someone who encourages others with words of kindness. Be someone who is merciful, compassionate, and quick to forgive. Be someone who understands others' pain and sees through others' behavior to the root of what's really going on in their lives. This is the mind of Christ. This is the Holy Spirit in action.

Have you ever been around someone who is humble, kind, and gentle? Their words exude encouragement, humility, and grace. You leave their presence feeling better than when you entered their presence. Your words either build people up or they tear them down. Decide to build others up. This is the way of Christ.

"A tree is identified by its fruit. If a tree is good, its fruit will be good. If a tree is bad, its fruit will be bad." [6]

Allow your heart to swell with love. The American Medical Association says to have a healthy heart you need to manage your blood pressure, be physically active, reduce your intake of processed foods, and maintain a healthy weight. [7] As much as that may be important from a physical standpoint, I know plenty of people who follow that regimen who are depressed, bored, anxious, and carry a cynical view of life. They have yet to find their life's purpose. Don't misunderstand me; I endorse a healthy physical lifestyle. I lead one myself. However, what's more important than a healthy lifestyle is a healthy heart that is focused on the eternal.

Give all your worries and cares to God, for he cares about you. [8]

God is the ultimate physician. He wants to mend your wounded heart, whether your wounds are self-inflicted or sustained from others. In order for healing to take place, God needs access to the inner chambers. He designed your heart to begin with, so He knows exactly what it needs to heal and thrive.

When you expose your heart and allow yourself to be vulnerable, your likelihood of being hurt increases. For this reason, people tend to build walls around their hearts to protect them. But as long as the walls are up around your heart, God cannot operate. When you trust God enough to open your heart to Him, He will mend your broken heart with love and care. God will not hurt you. He can fix anything that He sees that is out of place *or* He can give you *His* heart.

Can God heal a broken heart? Yes. God is capable of healing every part of your broken heart. However, His desire is to *replace* your heart with His heart. *"I will give you a new heart and put a new spirit in you; I will re-move from you your heart of stone and give you a heart of flesh."* [9] He wants to give you a non-surgical heart transplant. When you bring your used car with the check engine light on to a mechanic, would you prefer they fix it or replace it with a brand-new car? Choose to receive a new heart. Choose to receive God's heart. You won't regret it.

Mission Principle 17
Replace the treasure in your heart with the
treasure of God's Word.

PATH TO PROGRESS

Desire to store God's commands in your heart. *Proverbs 3:1*
Choose not to depend on your understanding. *Proverbs 3:5*
Decide to trust in God's laws. *Psalm 19:7*
The **result** is you will live in safety and prosperity. *Psalm 37:3*
The **promise** is understanding will protect you. *Proverbs 2:11*

Question from Jesus
"Why do you entertain evil thoughts in your hearts?" [10]

Questions to Meditate On
What is the health of your heart?
What are your heart's treasures?
What treasures do you need to add or remove from your heart?
Do your words build up or tear down?

Your Call to Action
Open your heart. Identify your treasures.
Remove the junk. Stockpile eternal treasures.

Day 18

ABSORB GOD'S WORD

For the word of God is living and powerful, and sharper than any two-edged sword, piercing even to the division of soul and spirit, and of joints and marrow, and is a discerner of the thoughts and intents of the heart. [1]

God's Word will satisfy your spirit and soul. It will always be more satisfying than anything this world can offer. When you fill up on God's Word early in the morning, you set up your day for success. You fill your heart up with joy, hope, love, peace, and understanding. God's knowledge permeates your heart, mind, and soul, equipping you to speak the truth and conquer the day. *Take the helmet of salvation and the sword of the Spirit, which is the word of God.* [2]

To *absorb* God's Word is to meditate on it daily. Stay focused by immersing yourself in His Word so it's etched on the walls of your heart. To gain knowledge is to gain understanding, and by gaining understanding, you will gain wisdom. The first step to gain knowledge is setting aside enough time each day to be silent before the Lord. Study the Scripture for the knowledge you need. By reading through God's Word on a consistent basis, you will discover the knowledge you need and how to apply it in your life. Memorize God's Word, so you will be able to recall the knowledge when the time comes to make wise decisions in your life and speak life into others.

The Bible is a treasure chest full of God's knowledge and wisdom waiting for you to open. Take out the treasures and share them with others in need. God's treasure was never meant to be buried; it was created for distribution. The treasure of the Bible is free for all to enjoy.

When you discover the treasure of eternal wisdom and knowledge in the Bible, don't keep it to yourself. By sharing the knowledge and giving the wisdom to others, you change lives, improve others' well-being, and create a currency that is able to be passed from generation to generation. *The law from your mouth is more precious to me than thousands of pieces of silver and gold.* [3]

We will not hide these truths from our children;
we will tell the next generation
about the glorious deeds of the LORD,
about his power and his mighty wonders. [4]

God's Word is the absolute truth. Once accepted, His Holy Spirit will provide you the understanding you need for complete revelation. The treasure chest of God's Word was created for all to participate in, for all to enjoy, for all to distribute and share amongst one another. It's an endless treasure chest. There are enough pieces to go around. Right when you come to the bottom, you discover another layer underneath the initial treasure chest. God's knowledge is inexhaustible.

By wisdom the LORD laid the earth's foundations,
by understanding he set the heavens in place. [5]

Wisdom was created before the beginning of time. It was the first thing God created. If you trust the Word of God, you trust that His supernatural wisdom is above your human wisdom. God's knowledge may seem foreign or even confusing the first time you read it. That is ok. The Holy Spirit will reveal everything at the right time. You will discover how to apply God's knowledge through your relationship with His Holy Spirit.

If you ask for insight, you will be heard. If you desire to gain knowledge, the roadmap will be provided. As you explore God's treasure chest, you will start to desire more and more knowledge. The Holy Spirit will continue to reveal to you how this knowledge can be applied to your everyday life. He will show you how to convert biblical knowledge to human understanding, which will result in wise decisions. *Cry out for insight, / and ask for understanding. [6] For wisdom will enter your heart, / and knowledge will fill you with joy. [7]*

Wisdom and knowledge precede joy. One of the greatest things about knowledge is that it comes packaged with joy. When you become a knowledgeable person, you become a joyful person, among other things. When you understand and accept God's ways and His promises, you will desire to pursue the path to fulfill God's will. You will be able to make solid, biblically based decisions that bring honor and glory to God. This will result in great joy in your heart and blessings in your life. God's wisdom is part of your defense against the evil in this world. Remember, the Word of God is sharper than any two-edged sword. [8]

But whose delight is in the law of the LORD,
and who meditates on his law day and night. [9]

God's Word is an incredible gift. It's His platform and subject matter to deepen your relationship with Him on a daily basis. Why do so few choose to explore God's treasure chest? Their Bible is tucked away in a drawer or on a bookshelf collecting dust. Yet all of life's choices, options, decisions, answers, and paths to progress are contained within the Bible.

If you dedicate the first hour of your day to reading the Word of God, your life will be transformed. Choose to spend time with Him and unlock the mystery of His Scripture. Absorb God's Word into your spirit. Continue the habit of seeking God's righteousness day after day. You will be crowned with God's glory. *The silver-haired head is a crown of glory, / it is found in the way of righteousness. [10]*

Make a decision today to begin meditating on the laws of the Lord day and night. It will be one of the best decisions you'll ever make in your lifetime. The moment you embrace the Bible as the wellspring of life that produces life-giving content better than any news station, podcast, blog, internet site, or newspaper, you will find the answers and rest you need. Meditate on God's promises by re-reading the words over and over again. Realize that God's Word is alive. It's incredible and understandable.

Mission Principle 18
Meditate on the words of God in the Bible every day.

Day 18

PATH TO PROGRESS

Desire to listen for and turn to wisdom. *Proverbs 2:2*
Choose to ask for understanding and call out for knowledge.
Proverbs 2:3
Decide to meditate on God's law day and night. *Psalm 1:2*
The **result** is you will bear much fruit. *Psalm 1:3*
The **promise** is God stores up wisdom for the righteous. *Proverbs 2:7*

Question from Jesus
*"Have you never read in the Scriptures:
'The stone the builders rejected / Has become the chief cornerstone. / This
was the LORD's doing, / And it is marvelous in our eyes'?"* [11]

Questions to Meditate On
Who or what do I turn to for knowledge?
How often do I read the Bible?
Do I seek answers to life's problems in the Bible?
Am I asking the Holy Spirit for better understanding?

Your Call to Action
Read the Bible daily. Meditate on the truths.
Ask the Holy Spirit questions. Absorb God's Word.

RESHAPE YOUR MIND

"It is what comes from inside that defiles you." [1]

Your natural inclination is to sin. To break that habit, you start by reshaping your mind. Your thought patterns need to change. Evil starts in your heart. It grows into your mind through seeing, hearing, or thinking about something sinful. If dwelt upon long enough, it will lead to temptation. If the temptation is acted on, it will create more sin. The cycle continues. You can break this pattern today by confessing the sin to God, sharing it with a trusted accountability partner, and seeking insight, wisdom, and knowledge through Scripture about how to overcome that sin in your life. *For it is better, if it is the will of God, to suffer for doing good than for doing evil.* [2]

The wicked conceive evil;
they are pregnant with trouble
and give birth to lies. [3]

Evil is a choice. Temptation seems to show itself most during those defining moments of choice in your life. After evil is devised, the mind has a way of justifying, blocking, and pretending what you just conceived is not actually evil. You can reason with yourself that what you are choosing to do is not really evil. You can come up with just about any excuse that justifies the evil you desire. In any case, regardless of the reason or justification, evil is born.

Deciding to do the right thing takes courage. It's so easy to choose *the easy way.* Doing it the right way many times means spending more time to do something properly. It may cost you money that you "don't have," but in the end, it's worth it. God promises to reward *just* behavior.

You serve a honest and just God. Focusing on His words and meditating on His Scriptures protects your mind. The more time you spend learning about the things of God, the healthier your mind will be. The more time you spend learning about things of the world, the more unhealthy your mind will be. You can easily bring on a light depression by habitually listening to the news cycle, reading the newspaper, or digesting other mainstream media outlets. Awareness of what's going on in the world around you is perfectly fine; however, when it becomes your primary source of information, it becomes a dangerous, slippery slope.

By waking up in the morning and immediately diving into social media, the news, or some other media outlet to find the latest breaking news, which is usually not positive, you have just compromised your mind-set for the day. It can eat up several hours of your day and leave you feeling anxious, uncertain, and hopeless. Or you can choose to start your day with Jesus and fill your mind with His words and promises. Spend time listening to others on the same pursuit of God's Word who seek to encourage and inspire you. This will fill your mind with positive ideas and hope for the future. Seek God's kingdom, model Jesus's ways, and watch what God does in your life.

Wake up and reach for the Word of God. When Jesus walked the earth, that's what He did. *Very early in the morning, while it was still dark, Jesus got up, left the house and went off to a solitary place, where he prayed.* [4] I believe He did this to get His mind-set right before the day began. You can take a similar approach. Avoid allowing negative thoughts and unhealthy inputs into your mind at the beginning of the day. By following Jesus's method, you will have a much more positive, uplifting day with the prospect of protection for your mind.

I come to you for protection, O LORD my God.
Save me from my persecutors—rescue me! [5]

If you desire the Lord to protect your mind, ask for His protection. If you do not seek His protection, you leave your mind open for attack.

By ignoring or rejecting God, you're raising your hand up high, putting your stake in the ground, and saying, "I got this, God; I don't need you right now. I'm going to handle this by myself." God's Word is called a shield throughout Scripture. Why is that? A shield is devised to protect, encompass, and block undesirable things that are coming at you. When you choose to use God's Word as your shield, you will be able to defend yourself from attacks that attempt to prevent you from fulfilling God's will.

My shield is God Most High,
who saves the upright in heart. [6]

Your mind is like a magnet. It attracts various elements, some better than others. Certain elements attach to the magnet of your mind. If you've ever tried to pull apart two magnetic parts, you realize how difficult it is. You're fighting the magnetic force. This is the same with your mind. When you allow something to attach to your mind that doesn't belong there, it becomes very hard to pull it off. You need to be renewed, cleansed, and washed. You have to intentionally introduce a new element that will diffuse the magnetic attachment that is currently in place.

Bathing in the Word of God will cleanse your mind. God's Word allows you to press the reset button daily. It will equip you in the morning with hope and instruction for the day and help wind you down in the evenings with God's promises to help you sleep in peace without worry.

When Jesus was on earth, He asked people questions, right on the spot, to help reshape their minds. He posed questions on a variety of topics that can still help today as you start to reshape your mind-set.

Jesus questions your memory to remind you of the truth.

+   *"Have I not chosen you?"* [7]
+   *"Did not the Messiah have to suffer these things and then enter his glory?"* [8]

+ *"What is written in the Law? ... How do you read it?"* [9]
+ *"Do you bring in a lamp to put it under a bowl or a bed? Instead, don't you put it on its stand?"* [10]
+ *"What did Moses command you?"* [11]

Jesus questions your fear to renew your strength.

+ *"Can any one of you by worrying add a single hour to your life?"* [12]
+ *"Why do you worry about clothes?"* [13]
+ *"Why are you so afraid? Do you still have no faith?"* [14]

Jesus questions your doubt to grow your confidence.

+ *"If I am telling the truth, why don't you believe me?"* [15]
+ *"If you do not believe his [Moses's] writings, how will you believe My words?"* [16]
+ *"I have spoken to you of earthly things and you do not believe; how then will you believe if I speak of heavenly things?"* [17]
+ *"Why are you troubled, and why do doubts rise in your minds?"* [18]
+ *"Where is your faith?"* [19]
+ *"Do you believe that I am able to do this?"* [20]
+ *"Why do you entertain evil thoughts in your hearts?"* [21]
+ *"Why did you doubt?"* [22]

Keep your mind focused on God. God looks deep within the mind and heart of every man and woman on earth. He knows your innermost thoughts and sees your actions even when you do them behind closed doors. Being omnipresent gives Him access to your most private life and thoughts. He knows your mind as He's the one who created your innermost parts. He knows what you think and how you think, even before you do.

You have searched me, LORD,
and you know me.
You know when I sit and when I rise;
you perceive my thoughts from afar.

You discern my going out and my lying down;
you are familiar with all my ways.
Before a word is on my tongue
you, LORD, know it completely. [23]

Ask God to reshape your thought patterns. If you've ever watched a scary or violent movie in the evening, you know you typically do not dream well later that night. Right before you go to sleep, if all the inputs into your mind are unhealthy, for the next several hours, your *rest* usually results in abnormal *wrestling*. On the contrary, if you fill your mind full of positive, uplifting images and thoughts right before you go to sleep, you will rest peacefully.

Retaining a healthy mind requires discipline. Your mind was designed to absorb, filter, and analyze information, then to express it back through ideas and your contribution to the world. To reshape your mind, don't focus on *changing your mind's thoughts;* instead, focus on *what thoughts you allow to enter your mind.* Read God's Word and put on "the mind of Christ" to be transformed today. [24]

Mission Principle 19
Filter your thoughts. Put on the mind of Christ.

Path to Progress

Desire the Lord's protection. *Psalm 7:1*
Choose not to conceive evil. *Psalm 7:14*
Decide to do the right thing. *1 Peter 3:17*
The **result** is God, the just and honest judge, will be your shield.
Psalm 7:10
The **promise** is God looks deep inside your mind and heart. *Psalm 7:9*

Question from Jesus
"Why are you thinking these things?" [25]

Questions to Meditate On
What positive inputs in your life are affecting your thought patterns?
What negative inputs in your life are affecting your thought patterns?
What are the aftereffects of those thoughts on the outputs of your life?
Do you control your thoughts or do your thoughts control you?

Your Call to Action
Put on the mind of Christ. Ask the Holy Spirit for help.
Meditate on biblical themes.

REDEFINE YOUR LIFE

"Seek the Kingdom of God above all else, and he will give you everything you need." [1]

Does your spiritual life need a total makeover? Today it's common-place to do a total makeover of your home, wardrobe, hair, and anything else in your world that needs a facelift. Why is doing a total makeover of *your spirit* out of the question? It's not. When you commit to a total makeover of your spirit, you create the opportunity to redefine your life's purpose, its pursuit, its goal, and its end game.

It works like this. If you are willing to redefine your life, you will have to redefine your purpose. While redefining your purpose, you will venture down a new path. To choose a new path, you will have to renew your decision-making process. If you choose the right path, it will lead you to desirable results. You can only accomplish these results by tapping into heavenly wisdom and understanding. These are the same two elements God used when He created the heavens and the foundations of the earth.

The LORD by wisdom founded the earth;
By understanding He established the heavens. [2]

Redefine your life by living for today and keeping a healthy perspective on tomorrow. The days of our lives are made up of a series of patterns, schedules, time frames, constrictions, and boundaries revolving around worldly pursuits. God's vision for your life shatters all of that. Start to redefine your life according to His perspective. A kingdom perspective. Jesus was not constrained to a pattern, schedule, or any other type of constriction or boundary.

Jesus knew no limits. He operated outside the everyday structure around Him. He redefined what life can be. In order for you to make use of your human understanding and truly uncover all the best jewels within God's treasure chest, you need to redefine your life. Follow Christ's example. He made healthy decisions through wisdom by seeking God's counsel.

Start to imagine a new life for yourself. Take a look at the boundaries in your life. Each of your boundaries has been set in place by yourself or others. Analyze your schedule. What are your priorities? If you redefine your life to be something beyond "normal," then the pattern of your behavior will need to change. What you're working toward will need to change. If you desire the life that God intended for you to live, which is *the more abundant life,* [3] you will have to redefine your interpretation of normal.

What is a *normal life?* In the world's perspective, a *normal life* could be defined as someone who is a contributing member of society, holds a college degree, is gainfully employed, has a family, saves for retirement, retires, does the things that they like for the tail end of their life, leads a good life, dies, has a well-attended funeral, is fondly remembered, and hopefully, goes to heaven.

Within the kingdom of God, a *normal life* can be defined as *someone who seeks God day and night.* Whether they attended college, held a successful job, or had a family with children is not what defines their allegiance or relevance. Their devotion to God is what defines them. Their relevance is whether or not they found and fulfilled God's will for their life. Was their number one priority to find and fulfill His will? Did they produce a harvest by leading individuals everywhere they went to the saving knowledge of Jesus Christ? Did they love others like Mother Teresa did? She understood what it meant to be a citizen of the kingdom of

God, relevant here on earth. Billy Graham, Martin Luther King Jr., and many other real-life saints are not remembered for their *normal lives* but for stepping up and doing something great to glorify God. They impacted the world in such a way that their reputations will live on for generations.

When Jesus was on earth, He asked people questions to help them think deeply about their lives. He questioned obedience to reveal loyalty, discernment to open eyes, and intentions to uncover motives. Jesus presented compelling questions to expose the heart. More of Jesus's questions are presented in Appendix 1.

Jesus questions your obedience to reveal your loyalty.

+ *"Why do you call me, 'Lord, Lord,' and do not do what I say?"* [4]
+ *"How will you escape being condemned to hell?"* [5]
+ *"Do you understand what I have done for you?"* [6]

Jesus questions your discernment to open your eyes.

+ *"Why do you look at the speck of sawdust in your brother's eye and pay no attention to the plank in your own eye?"* [7]
+ *"For who is greater, the one who is at the table or the one who serves?"* [8]
+ *"Did not the one who made the outside make the inside also?"* [9]

Jesus questions your intentions to uncover your motives.

+ *"What good will it be for someone to gain the whole world, yet forfeit their soul? Or what can anyone give in exchange for their soul?"* [10]
+ *"If you love those who love you, what reward will you get?"* [11]
+ *"Why are you thinking these things in your hearts?"* [12]

Redefine your life today. Start by spending time in God's Word reviewing the story and context behind each of Jesus's questions. Look at what decisions you've made in the past that impacted you positively and negatively and then make modifications moving forward. Learn from your past so history does not repeat itself. Be honest about your mistakes. Let go and forgive those who have hurt you. These are essential steps for you to move forward.

Work on redefining your life by defining what your purpose is. Every single person is capable of doing something to advance the kingdom of God. Study His blueprint. Access His divine knowledge. Make Him the treasure of your heart. Learn how to make wise decisions through God's wisdom. Choose the right path and decide to do something courageous.

Mission Principle 20
Redefine your life by asking yourself the right questions.

Day 20

Path to Progress

Desire to be aware and use better judgment. *Proverbs 4:1*
Choose to pursue wisdom and strengthen your good judgment.
Proverbs 4:5
Decide that wisdom's instructions are the key to life. *Proverbs 4:13*
The **result** is wisdom will make you great if you value it. *Proverbs 4:8*
The **promise** is wisdom will give you a good, long life. *Proverbs 4:10*

Question from Jesus
"Do you still not understand?" [13]

Questions to Meditate On
What is the one word that defines your life?
Do you believe that you can change what defines you?
Why do you believe you are here on earth?
What are you supposed to do with your life?

Your Call to Action
Believe it's possible. Confess your reality.
Find a new "normal." Redefine your life.

MISSION FINDER STORY
LETTING GO OF MY HEART'S TREASURE

With God, all things are possible. This proved true in my life after I graduated from high school, and I had an important decision to make. This was a defining moment in my life that would alter the course of my destiny. Should I attend college or chase my dreams to become a real estate entrepreneur? Against my parents' wishes and my financial well-being, I decided to pursue real estate. I will never forget the day my father called and said, "If you drop out of school, you are cut off financially."

"Fine!" I replied hastily as the phone went silent. I was eighteen years old.

Initially, I was upset with my parents, but upon reflection, I think it was one of the best decisions they ever made. It forced me to mature and taught me how to support myself at an early age. I grew up in a middle-class lifestyle, and my family lived within our means. I never knew what it was like to have abundant financial resources at my fingertips. I was intrigued by the lifestyle of the rich and famous and wondered what it was like to live that kind of lifestyle. Thus, my pursuit of "happiness" began.

During my childhood, my mother exemplified what it looked like to pursue God's will and do it. As a young boy, I gave my life to Christ with all that I understood at the time. However, at the age of thirteen I walked away from Him, thus ushering in the next phase of my life, which I aptly named The Lost Decade.

By my early twenties, I achieved my dreams of success by worldly standards and idolized my possessions. I fell victim to the deception of worldly riches: they became my heart's treasure. During my late twenties,

I was humbled as I realized I had gained success but had not attained fulfillment. My mother's influence continued to remind me of who I was in Christ. An unexpected influence that I believe was orchestrated by none other than my Lord and Savior was the woman I would later marry. I met her walking one day near the beach in La Jolla, California. She challenged me to pursue an intentional and strong relationship with God. These factors led me to surrender myself and ultimately all of my businesses to God. He has since opened doors I never dreamed of and bestowed many blessings, like my wife and children, all because of an act of surrender and obedience.

In 2004, I launched my real estate company, AARE. By God's grace, before the market crash of 2008, I decided to sell all of my real estate holdings to provide the capital necessary to start the company. What I treasured in my heart was beginning to change. My influence on others' lives and their well-being began to take precedence over my personal net worth and possessions. Little by little, the organization grew. Like a child, it went through its exciting developmental years, rocky teenage years, and calmer adult years to become the established company it is today, focused on God's will and carrying out His mission in the workplace.

I feel so blessed to lead a Christ-centered company that can lead people to witness the joys of a fully surrendered life. This is done through the platform of buying and selling real estate. Our mission as a company is to fulfill God's will. Our vision is to bear much fruit. We honor Him within our real estate agency by nurturing a culture where giving and serving others' needs before our own is a priority. We obey His Word by growing our business based on His moral, ethical, and biblical principles. Our core values include relationships, faith, accountability, integrity, natural and spiritual gifts, truth, honesty, trust, standards of excellence, generous giving, education, understanding, clear communication, work-life balance, morals, ethics, loyalty, gratefulness, biblical success, and rewards.

Upon reflection, I see that my heart's treasure as a young man was rooted in selfishness, monetary gain, and the vanity of worldly success. God helped me replace those treasures with a new treasure: His will. Over the course of two decades, God brought me full circle to the faith I once held as a young boy. As He walked with me through the peaks and valleys that were necessary for me to venture through, He revealed to me the emptiness of worldly wealth so I could let go of predefined success. His Son, Jesus, taught me how to pursue God's will, live in agreement with His commands, and be obedient to His ways.

step six

CHOOSE THE RIGHT PATH

WISDOM

REPURPOSE YOUR PURSUIT

Look to the LORD and his strength; seek his face always. [1]

Everyone is pursuing something. In that pursuit, you will find your identity and your purpose. Many pursue a path toward financial security and seek fulfillment by achieving a high net worth. Unfortunately, once they achieve financial security, they realize they are still not fulfilled. Pursuing financial security in this world can often mean sacrificing spiritual growth. You might ask, "Does pursuing the path toward financial security have *any* good purpose?" According to Jesus, the answer is no.

"Do not lay up for yourselves treasures on earth, where moth and rust destroy and where thieves break in and steal; but lay up for yourselves treasures in heaven, where neither moth nor rust destroys and where thieves do not break in and steal." [2]

Your time is precious. It's your most valuable asset. Is the majority of your time focused on accumulating things in this world that are only temporary and will pass away? Or are you focused on eternal treasure? If you refocus your attention on eternal treasures, you will start to repurpose your pursuit. You will come to the conclusion that God designed resources to be accumulated so that they can be redistributed. Using the knowledge, wisdom, and understanding of God's biblical principles, there is no doubt you can increase your financial resources. Then you will have a decision to make. What will you do with those resources? Will you follow the kingdom principle of stewardship or will you follow the world's way of accumulation?

"You will be my witnesses, telling people about me everywhere ... to the ends of the earth." [3]

Use your resources to share God's love worldwide. Through hard work and wisdom, you can grow your worldly resources. If you accumulate abundant resources, you have two choices. You can keep them for yourself or you can give them away. If you choose to give them away, you can turn your worldly resources into heavenly resources. Once God knows that He can trust you to do the right thing with worldly resources, He will equip you with everything you need so that you may bless others and distribute those resources throughout the world. That is, if you pursue a purpose based on kingdom principles. If you pursue a purpose solely for your *personal well-being* to become prosperous, gain wealth, and live in comfort, which are rooted in selfishness and accumulation, God will not bless that pursuit over the long term. You may experience windfalls of short-term accumulation; however, in my experience, God uses these windfalls to teach His children a lesson about long-term stewardship and generosity.

That person is like a tree planted by streams of water,
which yields its fruit in season
and whose leaf does not wither—
whatever they do prospers. [4]

God wants you to thrive in all that you do. He wants to develop your character. Your contribution to the process is being obedient to His Word. God cannot develop your character when you are disobedient. He cannot help you develop your spiritual character when you are in disagreement with His laws and His Word. God is a *just* God. God is a *holy* God. God cannot bend His own rules. If you seek spiritual growth in your life, simply follow God's guidelines. He will never let you down.

Watch out for the prosperity gospel. There are many preachers who preach what's called a "prosperity gospel," which basically says if you give money to the church, God will give you more money in return and that's why you should give money. That's a false gospel. God commands you to *tithe* out of obedience to Him, meaning to give ten percent of your gross income. On top of that, if you are led, you can give over and above your tithe. This is called *an offering* to God.

God promises that He will honor those gifts you are offering to Him. God promises that He will fill your storehouse beyond measure. He may choose to fill your storehouse in a different way than further financial gain, though. He actually says "test me" in Scripture: *"Test me in this,"* *says the LORD Almighty, "and see if I will not throw open the floodgates of heaven and pour out so much blessing that there will not be room enough to store it."* [5]

I took God up on that test twelve years ago. At the time, I considered myself to be a sharing person who liked to help and bless others. Upon reflection, I now recognize my self-centeredness. Although I was sharing and giving to others around me, it also benefited me in some way or another. I was not being obedient to God's Word. I was giving a little here, a little there, but nothing substantial or consistent toward what God cares about.

In 2009, all of that changed. During the midst of an economic crisis, I felt compelled to give away $2,000 to a ministry called Formando Vidas in Colombia, which helps street children in the inner city of Bogota. My heart was moved by the great need I witnessed firsthand. In that moment, I expressed a *desire*, then made a *choice* followed by a *decision* to become a more generous giver. I set an initial goal to give away $10,000 as soon as possible. After that was accomplished, I expressed to God my desire to give away $100,000. Then $1 million. Most recently, I expressed my desire to God to give away $100 million. When God fulfills my desire, if He so chooses, I will express my desire to give more. In reality, I am simply giving back to God what He gave me in the first place.

When I expressed my initial desire to become more generous, I had no clue how I was going to make an extra $10,000 or $100,000 to give away on top of earning enough to pay the bills. I live in California where the average lifestyle is expensive by any measure. God heard my request and responded. I expressed my desire through prayer until He showed me the way to earn the money so that I could give it right back to His purposes. I discovered stewarding money requires a lot of time and responsibility.

The same story unfolded when I decided I wanted to give away $1 million. I didn't know how it was all going to come together, but it started with me expressing a desire. I faithfully worked hard and prayed over that desire consistently. I put it in print so there was no going back. Then, I announced it to a room full of colleagues for accountability. I did everything I could to set up my goal for success from inception by following the instructions of the Bible. I started by praying privately, as instructed by God's Scripture: *"But when you give to the needy, do not let your left hand know what your right hand is doing, so that your giving may be in secret. Then your Father, who sees what is done in secret, will reward you."* [6]

The only cure to selfishness and greed is generosity. Through studying God's divine design on a daily basis, I am constantly reminded of Jesus's example of selflessness and generosity. I stay focused on the radical results Jesus produced through His righteous acts. Today is no different from the first day I expressed my initial desire to become more generous. I find myself right where I began my journey of generosity, not knowing how it's all going to work but trusting God. I know that if I align my desires and will with His, I will succeed. I know if I use my gifts and talents for God's glory, He will carve a path and lead the way to make my desire a reality.

"And when you pray, do not be like the hypocrites, for they love to pray standing in the synagogues and on the street corners to be seen by others. Truly I tell you, they have received their reward in full." [7]

God continues to walk with me every step of the way on my journey of generosity. Temptation will always exist as I'm still faced with the same selfish temptations as I was twelve years ago when I began my journey of generosity. My response to that temptation is now controlled by the Holy Spirit who resides inside of me. I still have to make sound choices followed by wise decisions that translate to positive results. This is true for my giving and everything else in my life. There are moments in my life when I'm tempted to be self-centered, disobedient to God, and to not honor my commitments. Like most, I am tempted to be self-serving and to keep more for myself than I need.

One day, I discovered how many people in the world are still living without God's Word in their primary language. That changed my life forever. I decided to repurpose my pursuit on the spot.

"And this gospel of the kingdom will be preached in all the world as a witness to all the nations, and then the end will come." [8]

You have the privilege to fulfill this biblical prophecy. What an honor it is to be an ambassador of Jesus Christ in this day and age. When Christ spoke this prophecy into existence, it opened all types of doors for believers worldwide. Prior to Christ's initial coming to earth, worldwide travel was uncommon. Boats could take you from port to port, but that was about it. Over the last two thousand years, the world has experienced dramatic advances in transportation. Although the titans of the industrial and technological revolutions attempt to take credit, I believe based on His Word that God poured out the wisdom and knowledge on humanity so that *His* mission of reaching every tribe and every nation could be accomplished. [9]

Two of my friends who have *repurposed their pursuits* are Todd Peterson and Mart Green. Todd's initial pursuit in life was to be in the NFL. He fulfilled that pursuit. Mart's initial pursuit in life was to help his family build Hobby Lobby and to build his own personal business, Mardel Christian and Education stores. He fulfilled those purposes. Both Todd and Mart sought something more eternal once their initial pursuits in life were fulfilled. They sought to find and fulfill God's will for their lives. God revealed it in a major way. Today, Todd and Mart lead an alliance of organizations called illumiNations. [11] The mission of illumiNations is to eradicate Bible poverty.

What is Bible poverty, you ask? Living in Bible poverty is being part of a people group with little or no access to Scripture in your *heart* language. Your *heart* language is the language that means the most to you. It's the language that resonates the deepest within your soul. Believe it or not, there are more than six thousand living languages that are spoken today. [11] Approximately two thousand of these have adequate Scripture, two thousand are in the process—and two thousand don't have a single verse of Scripture.

Imagine waking up each morning trying to read God's precious words in a foreign language. This should be a top priority mission to complete for the entire Christian community. IllumiNations helps orchestrate the co-ordination of the ten leading Bible translation agencies worldwide with a goal to see Scripture translated for all those living in Bible poverty by 2033. They are on their way to completing their mission. Todd and Mart—and their spouses Susan and Diana—have utilized their gifts and talents toward eternal kingdom investments by repurposing their pursuits to fulfill God's will.

But whose delight is in the law of the LORD,
and who meditates on his law day and night. [12]

Help overcome Bible poverty by spreading God's laws and wisdom. Embrace God's laws and help share His wisdom. By analyzing the laws of the Lord, accepting them, loving them, and delighting in them, you embrace His divine wisdom. This is what God desires. He created His laws for your well-being. He designed them to be shared with others. He didn't design His laws to hurt you. He designed His laws to keep your life in order. Learn to love His laws and apply them in your life. Understanding His laws gives you the ability to utilize them as you navigate through life. Rejoicing in His laws is part of your life's mission.

*Their [proverbs'] purpose is to teach people wisdom and discipline,
to help them understand the insights of the wise.* [13]

How do you make wise decisions? By applying insight, knowledge, and discernment. These are the three things that come before a wise decision. First, you attain the proper insight into a situation and take a look at all the alternatives and risk factors. Next, you gather knowledge and information about that particular decision. Finally, you need to be able to filter and discern between all the available options to arrive at a wise decision.

*Let the wise listen to these proverbs and become even wiser.
Let those with understanding receive guidance.* [14]

The good news is there is a manual to life with all the wisdom that you seek waiting for you to open the book and spend time on a daily basis learning how to make wise decisions. The magnificent book of Proverbs in the Bible contains 15,038 words of wisdom inside 915 verses wrapped up in 31 chapters, one for each day of the month. If you seek wisdom, read Proverbs.

By reading and memorizing Jesus's parables, the Proverbs, and words of the wise, *you* will become wise. Too many Christians are so concerned with being "wise in their own eyes" that they choose not to pursue the wisdom found within the Bible at all. Afraid of being *judged* by others, they prefer to keep things light and keep deep conversation to a minimum out of fear of sounding like a Bible fanatic. The desire to avoid an argument or conflict prevents deep, healthy wisdom from being nurtured and grown within one's spirit. Avoid letting the impression of being "wise in your own eyes" stop you from seeking wisdom.

Wisdom was made to be experienced. You are provided with choices every single day that can reshape your path. No one woke up suddenly wise. Wisdom comes through trial and error. Wisdom comes through experiments and failure. Wisdom comes by making mistakes. Wisdom comes from exploring stories and information from those who have come before you. God provides all the information you need at the exact time you need it in order to make good choices. Yielding to the Holy Spirit's direction will help guide you to determine the right decisions. Remember that good choices always precede a wise decision.

Mission Principle 21
Pursue the right path. Fulfill biblical prophecy.

Day 21

PATH TO PROGRESS

Desire insight, knowledge, and discernment to make wise decisions.
Proverbs 1:2
Choose to increase your wisdom and understanding by exploring
parables, proverbs, and words of the wise. *Proverbs 1:5-6*
Decide not to turn away from God's wisdom or instructions.
Proverbs 4:2
The **result** is wisdom will teach you straight paths. *Proverbs 4:11*
The **promise** is common sense and discernment will keep you safe on
your path. *Proverbs 3:21-23*

Question from Jesus
"What do you want?" [15]

Questions to Meditate On
What is your primary pursuit in life?
Does your primary pursuit draw you closer to God?
Which pursuits in your life draw you away from God?
What do you believe God wants you to pursue?

Your Call to Action
Review your lifestyle. Compare it with God's will.
Rearrange your priorities. Repurpose your pursuit.

Day 22

REARRANGE YOUR PRAYER LIFE

Hear my cry for help,
my King and my God,
for to you I pray.
In the morning, LORD, you hear my voice;
in the morning I lay my requests before you
and wait expectantly. [1]

The way to improve your life is to reprioritize your prayers. Solomon was the wisest man to ever live. In all his wisdom, he made one of the best decisions in human history. He decided to ask God for knowledge and understanding to lead his people to serve God, rather than request blessings for his own personal benefit. For this prayer, God blessed him with the wisdom and knowledge he requested plus abundant financial resources, making him the wealthiest individual who ever lived.

"Give me wisdom and knowledge, that I may lead this people, for who is able to govern this great people of yours?"

God said to Solomon, "Since this is your heart's desire and you have not asked for wealth, possessions or honor, nor for the death of your enemies, and since you have not asked for a long life but for wisdom and knowledge to govern my people over whom I have made you king, therefore wisdom and knowledge will be given you. And I will also give you wealth, possessions and honor, such as no king who was before you ever had and none after you will have." [2]

God listens to every one of your prayers. The question is, Are you listening to God? Are your prayers centered around your purposes or His?

While Jesus was here on earth, He set the model example in the Lord's Prayer. Have you studied the sequence of the Lord's Prayer? If not, spend time in the Word learning the method of how Jesus prayed.

If the desire, context, substance, or foundation of your prayer is not aligned with God's will, you run the risk of your prayer being unanswered. I have yet to meet an individual who has prayed for God's will in their life and had it not come to fruition. I've met thousands of individuals who are pursuing their own will and pray on a daily basis, yet their prayers go unanswered. I believe the reason they don't come to fulfillment is because they are based on self-interest.

For the flesh desires what is contrary to the Spirit, and the Spirit what is contrary to the flesh. They are in conflict with each other, so that you are not to do whatever you want. [3]

How should you approach God in prayer? God's Word teaches you how to approach Him by praying in the spirit. One of the main battles within our hearts comes from living in the flesh instead of living in the spirit. When you live in the flesh, your moment by moment concentration revolves around you. Your awareness is focused on how your mind, body, and senses feel. When you live in the spirit, your moment by moment concentration revolves around God. You are aware of God's presence and His interaction within your life. When you live in the spirit, you can properly access and utilize God's mercy, blessing, and direction to fulfill His will.

How do you receive God's mercy and blessing? It starts with your prayer requests aligning with His desires, not yours. No prayer is more redundant than requesting God to bless you in one way or the other. This is what I refer to as the request to bless prayer. Every day, God hears your personal request to bless prayers. I'm sure it makes Him smile, but it also makes Him shake His head. Why? Because He's given you all the instruction that you need within His Scripture in order to receive His blessings. While living in the flesh, you can pray until you're blue in the face for your requests to bless, but until you start following His direction, seeking His instruction, and obeying His commands, don't be surprised if you don't see His will come to pass. *"We are witnesses of these things, and so is the Holy Spirit, whom God has given to those who obey him."* [4]

If you were to put every human being's prayers worldwide into a pie chart, this is how I believe it would break down:

3% thanking God
3% praising God
3% questioning God
1% asking for forgiveness
90% requests to bless

When you pray using this format, you have the Lord's Prayer upside down. You put your temporal earthly requests above His eternal heavenly mandates. Your requests to bless should not be self-focused.

Therefore we also pray always for you that our God would count you worthy of this calling, and fulfill all the good pleasure of His goodness and the work of faith with power, that the name of our Lord Jesus Christ may be glorified in you, and you in Him, according to the grace of our God and the Lord Jesus Christ. [5]

Your top prayer requests should focus on heavenly priorities, in the proper order. Your requests should be the eight things that Jesus told you to pray about within the Lord's Prayer.

1. Praise and thanksgiving to God's holy name.
2. God's kingdom to come soon.
3. God's will to be done on earth as it is in heaven.
4. Provision for your daily bread.
5. Forgiveness for your sin.
6. Forgiving others who sin against you.
7. Not falling into temptation.
8. Keeping you safely away from Satan.

"Pray like this:
Our Father in heaven,
may your name be kept holy (1).
May your Kingdom come soon (2).
May your will be done on earth,
as it is in heaven (3).
Give us today the food we need (4),
and forgive us our sins (5),
as we have forgiven those who sin against us (6).
And don't let us yield to temptation (7),
but rescue us from the evil one (8)." [6]

Your primary request as a member of the body of Christ should be for the Holy Spirit to have paramount authority in your life. *Ask God* for His divine enlightenment and wisdom on how to carry out His will. *Ask God* for the opening of your heart so that He can repair and heal your wounds—emotionally, spiritually, and physically—so you can properly complete your mission. *Ask God* for understanding to make your marriage stronger or, if you are single, to prepare your heart, mind, and soul so that God can reveal the spouse He created for you. *Ask God* for the knowledge to disciple others more effectively. *Ask God* for a bountiful harvest, that many would come to know Him as their personal Lord and Savior. *Ask God* for an increase in the laborers of the field, that more would step up to bring in the harvest. Once these key heavenly mandates have been prayed for, with sincerity, you can move on to your temporal earthly requests. Jesus explained that God already knows your needs and will gladly provide to those who seek His will. *"Do not be like them, for your Father knows what you need before you ask him."* [7]

Other ways Jesus instructed us to pray in the Gospels include:
+ Pray in private, behind closed doors by yourself. [8]
+ When you pray, ask in Jesus's name. [9]
+ When you pray, begin by forgiving anyone you are holding on to anger toward, so God will forgive your sins, too. [10]
+ You can pray directly to God using the name of Jesus. [11]

* You can pray for anything, and if you have faith you've received it, it will be granted. [12]
* Ask anything in Jesus's name and He will do it. [13]
* If you ask, you will receive. If you seek, you will find. And if you knock, the door will be opened. [14]
* Your heavenly Father gives good gifts to people who ask Him. [15]

In the garden of Gethsemane, the night before He died, Jesus prayed for you and me. He prayed a *request to bless* prayer. However, it was not for His personal benefit. It was for your benefit. It was for my benefit. It was for the benefit of humankind. Listen to His heart. His focus was on others. Jesus prayed to His Father:

* Glorify me so I can glorify you. [16]
* Bring me into the glory you and I shared before creation. [17]
* Keep my followers safe from Satan. [18]
* Make my followers holy through your truth. [19]
* Teach my followers the truth, which is found in your word. [20]

Jesus also told you not to repeat yourself while praying. *"And when you pray, do not keep on babbling like pagans, for they think they will be heard because of their many words."* [21] God says that you can ask for anything when two are gathered. He will hear that request, and He will honor that request. *"Again I say to you that if two of you agree on earth concerning anything that they ask, it will be done for them by My Father in heaven."* [22]

Follow Jesus's example and His instructions in your prayer life. Find a prayer partner and start to pray for God's will to be fulfilled in both of your lives. Begin today.

Mission Principle 22
Rearrange your prayer requests to reflect
heavenly mandates.

Day 22

Path to Progress

Desire for the Lord to hear your prayers and listen to your cries and requests. *Psalm 5:1-3*
Choose to worship Him with deep awe. *Psalm 5:7*
Decide to love the name of God. *Psalm 5:11*
The **result** is God alone will be your inheritance and cup of blessing. *Psalm 16:5*
The **promise** is God will answer your prayer. *Psalm 17:6*

Question from Jesus
"What do you want me to do for you?" [22]

Questions to Meditate On
Are your prayers focused on your needs or God's will?
What blessings do you wish to receive from God?
What prayer is most close to God's heart?
What should you change about your prayer life?

Your Call to Action
Understand God's heart. Analyze your *requests to bless.*
Rearrange your prayer list. Repave your path.

Day 23

CALIBRATE YOUR DECISIONS
WITH WISDOM

Trust in the LORD with all your heart,
And lean not on your own understanding. [1]

Every day you are presented with life-changing choices. What you decide to do with those choices is what separates your life experience from others'. God instructs you to cross-reference your choices with His Word to figure out what the characters of the Bible did when presented with similar scenarios. By making your decisions based on His Word, you ensure that you are following God's divine design. Let God's wisdom, which has stood the test of time, shape your decisions. This means your role is to absorb the information, reshape your thinking patterns, and prepare to redefine your life.

As you start to rely on God's wisdom, you begin to realize how little you really know. This is part of opening your heart to God. Study God's incredible wisdom and approach Him with humility. Your understanding of His principles will thrive. Why depend on the world's information when you have access to divine knowledge? Let God change your heart and lead you down the right path. Cross-reference the Bible to ensure that your decisions are lining up with God's divine design. Simply put— let God be the chief decision maker in your life.

Trust in the LORD, and do good;
Dwell in the land, and feed on His faithfulness. [2]

You were designed to be fulfilled. Your whole life you have been placing things inside your heart, attempting to find satisfaction. There is only one thing that can give you everlasting fulfillment—faith in God.

Common wisdom says that addiction is a bad thing. Why is it that humans have a tendency to become addicted to something? We are seeking fulfillment. God designed us so that we would be fulfilled by Him. He designed us so that we would center our heart, praise, and worship around Him. He designed us to never stop needing His love, wisdom, mercy, and grace. There is such a thing as a healthy addiction that leads to everlasting fulfillment. His name is Jesus Christ.

If you aren't being fulfilled by Jesus, you will constantly be running on empty. How do you currently make your decisions? Do you consult advisors, your spouse, and those you trust? When life presents you with a fork in the road, you may ask yourself ... What would Jesus do? Jesus would ask His Father. You don't ever have to worry about making the wrong choice when you seek the Father's wisdom. You have His guidebook, His instruction manual for life, at your fingertips. You have to read it and know it through and through. Keep your Bible within reach at all times. Never leave home without it. A defining moment in my life was when I made the choice to document all of Jesus's promises one by one. Then, I decided to study how to obey the Word of God. One choice and one decision had a profound impact on my long-term spiritual well-being.

"I [wisdom] love those who love me,
And those who seek me diligently will find me." [3]

Aim for bullseye. When you make the decision to love wisdom, you open up the door to recalibrate your decision-making process. If you've ever shot a gun that's not properly calibrated, you realize that no matter how hard you try, you're not going to be able to hit the bullseye on the target. The same can be said when making decisions without wisdom. If your decision-making is off, your results will always be off. When you begin to value wisdom, the likelihood of hitting the bullseye increases tenfold.

*"For those who find me [wisdom] find life
and receive favor from the LORD."* [4]

If you desire God's favor in your life, seek wisdom. Wisdom precedes favor. Wisdom and God's favor are like brother and sister. We all want God's favor in our lives, but how do you find wisdom? You will find wisdom in the Bible through knowledge and understanding. By accessing God's divine knowledge and calling out for understanding, you will make wise decisions through His wisdom. Once you find God's wisdom, God's favor will follow.

When you seek knowledge, understanding is soon to follow. God knows that once you start seeking His knowledge, not your knowledge or the world's knowledge, He can trust you. Once your heart is aligned with His, God knows that you will administer His favor toward the things that He is most passionate about.

*Fear of the LORD is the foundation of true knowledge,
but fools despise wisdom and discipline.* [5]

Embrace discipline. Discipline keeps you healthy. It keeps your life balanced. You cannot have wisdom without discipline. Wisdom and discipline go hand in hand just like wisdom and favor. A rebellious person rejects discipline and, therefore, rejects wisdom. The fastest way to make poor decisions in your life is to despise wisdom and discipline. The results are never favorable. Once you accept discipline as a positive thing in your life, you open your heart to the possibility of wisdom reshaping your life.

*Wise choices will watch over you.
Understanding will keep you safe.* [6]

Your wise choices will watch over you just as God watches over you. When you make choices that align with God's will, you can rest assured that those choices will keep you safe. When you follow God's commands, your decisions are recalibrated to bring Him honor. Wise choices will watch over you. When you use the Bible to make your decisions, you have a benchmark to base all your decisions upon. The result of these decisions has been proven for thousands of years. You don't need to question whether the decision is going to work. If choices, decisions, and wisdom within the Bible didn't work, no one would subscribe to the Christian faith. God's Word produces incredible results. Give it an opportunity to transform your life.

Throughout the Gospels, Jesus illustrates cause and effect. He shows you with heavenly insight how your choices and decisions directly impact your life and eternal well-being. More examples are listed in Appendix 1.

+ *"The words you say will either acquit you or condemn you."* [7]
+ *"Your faith has made you well."* [8]
+ *"Anything is possible if a person believes."* [9]
+ *"Everyone who acknowledges me [Jesus] publicly here on Earth, I will also acknowledge before my Father in heaven."* [10]
+ *"For if you forgive other people when they sin against you, your heavenly Father will also forgive you."* [11]
+ *"Whoever feeds on this bread [Jesus] will live forever."* [12]
+ *"Anyone who believes in me [Jesus] will do the same works I have done, and even greater works."* [13]
+ *"Those who exalt themselves will be humbled, and those who humble themselves will be exalted."* [14]

Recalibrate your decision-making process by seeking wisdom daily. If you've made a habit of ignoring God's wisdom or seeking worldly wisdom from the internet, news, or any other source more than God's knowledge, stop that pattern today. Put down social media. Turn off the news. Throw away the newspaper. Open up the Bible. Start reading divine knowledge. Ask the Holy Spirit for understanding. God will reveal His wisdom. With God's wisdom, you will make wise decisions that will lead you to God's favor.

Mission Principle 23
Use God's wisdom to make your decisions.

Day 23

PATH TO PROGRESS

Desire to become wise. *Psalm 19:7*
Choose not to despise wisdom and discipline. *Proverbs 1:7*
Decide to love wisdom and pursue it. *Proverbs 8:17*
The **result** is when you find wisdom, you will also find life and receive
God's favor. *Proverbs 8:35*
The **promise** is your wise choices will protect you. *Proverbs 2:11*

Question from Jesus
"How will you escape being condemned to hell?" [15]

Questions to Meditate On
Are you seeking wisdom from people or from God?
Do you study Proverbs on a regular basis?
Are you seeking God's Word before making big decisions?
What life decisions would you change?

Your Call to Action
Call out to wisdom. Listen intently.
Wait patiently. Calibrate your decisions.

REVEAL RADICAL RESULTS

"And everyone who has left houses or brothers or sisters or father or mother or wife or children or fields for my sake will receive a hundred times as much and will inherit eternal life." [1]

Jesus led a radical life. You have the ability to live that same radical life. You can have all the wisdom in the world, but if that wisdom is rooted in worldly desires, then you're going to get worldly results. Instead, seek heavenly wisdom. This will lead you to do radical things for God's kingdom. This will present situations for you to earn one hundred times your original investment of time, money, or anything else of value that you give up for Christ's sake. To participate in these radical returns, simply choose the path of righteousness. Follow Jesus. If Jesus was a radical risk taker, why are modern-day Christians so determined to be conservative?

Christ pays radical dividends when you go "all in." Nearly twenty years ago, I invested in a real estate property in La Jolla, California. I used my real estate license, the commission due, and my negotiating skills to pay $10,000 cash as a down payment on a $550,000 purchase. The result was a twenty-five-fold return within nine months. I sold the property for $850,000 and cashed out a profit of $250,000 after my selling expenses. Percentage wise, it was one of the best investments of my lifetime.

Upon reflection, what I did with those proceeds may have been one of my worst expenditures of all time. Most of it was spent on worldly things. At the time, I thought I'd just won the lottery. I earned twenty-five times my original capital in a very short period of time. If you ask any investor, including myself, how many investments they are aware of that return one hundred times the initial investment, the number would be slim to none. In today's world, investors are content with a three to five percent return on their investments. One hundred times in return, as Christ promises, is nearly a ten thousand percent return. Those are radical results.

Imagine if you could invest $1 in something and get $100 back. You would put all your money into that investment immediately. The world financial system sells us on doing the polar opposite. It requires that we put $100 into an investment, and we hope that we get $3 to $5 extra back, equaling a three to five percent return. Why in the world would anyone invest their hard-earned $100 to try to squeeze out $3 to $5 more when you can invest your hard-earned $100 and receive $10,000 in heavenly currency?

Despite the common ideas that "it's all going to burn" and "you can't take any of it with you," I am here to tell you that is not true. You can take it with you if you invest in eternal kingdom investments. Giving up something of value that you treasure in exchange for doing something great in the world that will impact your eternal future and others' eternal futures is an investment that's worthwhile and logical.

Time is your most valuable asset. Now let's apply the one hundred times return principle to your time spent here on earth pursuing God's will for your life. Where do you spend the majority of your time? Likely at work. If you could invest ten hours of work time to receive one thousand hours of play time, would you do it? Of course you would. When you give your time to kingdom pursuits, God will free up more of your time to bear even more fruit. Christ assures you that anything you give up of value for His sake will be returned one-hundred-fold.

So you may walk in the way of goodness,
And keep to the paths of righteousness. [2]

Stay on the path of righteousness for the rest of your life. It's a choice. If you want to reveal radical results in your life, you will have to stay on the straight and narrow path. This is challenging to do on your own. The path of righteousness requires focus and awareness of anything that would try to draw you away from staying on that path.

For the LORD gives wisdom;
From His mouth come knowledge and understanding. [3]

Only God grants heavenly wisdom. Even the smartest person on the planet needs divine wisdom to navigate the world's challenges. You can download almost all the information in the world through the internet, yet little of that information will do you any good eternally. If you want to reshape your life and change the world, you will need God's wisdom. God is the one who grants that wisdom. The good news is that your relationship with Him, through your intimacy with Him, allows you to place a request for heavenly wisdom through prayer, which comes to us through the Holy Spirit.

If the only wisdom you acquire is *internal* wisdom from this world, you will be greatly limited. By seeking heavenly wisdom, which is *eternal*, you are petitioning the king of kings to deliver you divine wisdom, which is unmatchable. This is the type of wisdom that reshapes your life and the lives of those around you. Heavenly wisdom is imparted to us by the Almighty One, and it is He alone who gives the type of wisdom and understanding that can move mountains.

Here is a different take on the Big Bang theory. The *big* was God; the *bang* was wisdom. When those two powerful forces came together, Planet Earth was the result. It was not a *cosmic accident* but rather a *heavenly incident.* If God founded the earth based on wisdom, do you think it's important to use wisdom in your life? When wisdom enters your heart, you will know what is right, what is just, and which way to go. This is the relationship with wisdom God desires you to seek. One where wisdom, through the Holy Spirit, can control your life. And your decisions. *The LORD by wisdom founded the earth; / By understanding He established the heavens.* [4]

Give God's wisdom the respect it deserves. If God used wisdom as the foundation of the earth, it only makes sense to use wisdom as the foundation of your life. You can have a relationship with wisdom just like you have a relationship with God. You can call out to wisdom; you can ask questions of wisdom; you can put in requests, and wisdom will answer. As you start to align your heart with God's heart, you have to remove the worldly wisdom in your heart. This makes room in your heart for God to put in His wisdom, which you need to carry out your mission.

This leads us to the final part of our journey, which is to complete your mission. Now that you have chosen to make wise decisions with *God's wisdom*, the next step is to fulfill God's will and complete your mission by never giving up.

Mission Principle 24
Be prepared to take radical risks if you want radical results.

Day 24

PATH TO PROGRESS

Desire common sense, insight, and strength.
You will find them and wisdom. *Proverbs 8:14*
Choose to continue on the path of righteousness. *Proverbs 2:20*
Decide it is God who gives wisdom and ask Him for it. *Proverbs 2:6*
The **result** is wisdom will reside in your heart. You will know what is
right, just, and fair, and you will know the right path. *Proverbs 2:9*
The **promise** is by wisdom God founded the earth. *Proverbs 3:19*

Question from Jesus
"Where is your faith?" [5]

Questions to Meditate On
What risks in your life are you avoiding?
Is that avoidance preventing you from fulfilling God's will?
Are you depending on God for your safety or worldly security?
Are you investing in kingdom investments?

Your Call to Action
Protect your time. Take risks.
Seek God's shelter. Reveal radical results.

MISSION FINDER STORY
CHOOSING TO BE PRESENT

Life-transforming opportunities go unnoticed all the time—when you are too busy or too self-absorbed, even in doing good work, that you miss the people God is placing on your path. Every day, God presents you with divine appointments that can mark a significant milestone in your spiritual journey and the journey of those you meet. These opportunities are easy to miss if you are not paying attention. Has that ever happened to you? Years ago, after attending The Gathering conference in Florida, I could have missed two divine appointments had I not made two key choices.

Choosing to be present: The conference had come to a close, and a sense of excitement overwhelmed my spirit. It had been a magical week. The teaching, the music, the sharing, the giving, the laughter, the hope, the conviction, the prayers, and the inspiration that came by gathering with a group of warm-hearted, heavenly minded souls was infectious. The joy had woven deep into my spirit. I was elated. Now it was time to return to life as usual. I had a seven o'clock flight the next morning, so I went to bed early. The five o'clock wake-up call came fast. I jumped out of bed, got ready, headed for the lobby, and grabbed a newspaper on the way out of the hotel.

Still waking up, I hailed a cab and faced the first key choice on my drive to the airport. "Open your tablet and catch up with your emails," said the practical voice in my head. "Be present, talk to the driver, and share Christ," whispered a gentle voice in my spirit. "I may never see this person again," I countered back in my head. Isn't it amazing how fast we can switch gears from a heightened spiritual state to a pragmatic mind-set?

The driver was full of smiles, a Haitian refugee named Jack. By choosing to put my tablet down, I learned about Jack's life. For the last twenty years, he had built homes. Now he was driving cabs. He had a remarkable sense of pride for his work. I liked him immediately. He inquired about my trip to Florida. I shared the details of the conference with him. We spoke around the word Christianity for half of the ride. Then the word *Jesus* entered the conversation.

"Oh … you believe in Jesus," he said. "Now you are speaking my language."

"Tell me what Jesus has done in your life," I asked.

"I would have to drive you from Florida to California to explain all of the wonderful things God has done in my life," he replied. "I can't even begin to scratch the surface." After an inspiring conversation for the duration of the ride to the airport, I jumped out of the car and gave Jack a hug. "Please don't forget me" were his final words.

Choosing to raise my hand: As I was saying goodbye to Jack, I seriously considered canceling my flight and hiring him to drive me from Florida to California. I really wanted to hear the rest of his testimony. But I'm glad I didn't. My next divine appointment was awaiting me within the airport.

Have you ever felt like once you check your Good Samaritan box for the day, you can finally get back to your business at hand? That was my feeling as I entered the airport. I had given Jack half an hour of my time. Now I was ready to go into *flight mode*, put on my headphones, and fade away into my emails, my newspaper, and *my time*. As I approached the ticket counter, a young man was standing to my left. He was wearing a cut-off tank top and a sideways hat with the word *Mob* on it, and he had a stuffed animal strapped around his back.

I was about ready to swipe my card at the self-check kiosk for my extra bags when I heard the young man explain to the clerk next to me why he was short five dollars for his bag. He had just checked out of a drug treatment center and only had $20 cash to his name. "Could you give me some grace?" he asked the clerk.

"We're not a charity," the clerk responded.

"Excuse me," I said as I raised my hand to get the clerk's attention. I could not believe his rudeness and lack of sympathy. "I would like to pay for his bag along with mine."

The clerk's forehead scrunched up as he shook his head. The look of disbelief and annoyance was written all over his face. "You should give this nice man the twenty dollars since he's putting your luggage on his credit card," he said to the young man with contempt.

"That won't be necessary," I said. "Consider it a gift."

"Thank you! My name is Jose," said the young man, extending his hand to shake mine. As we walked toward the security checkpoint, I learned that he was heading to Los Angeles.

"Tell me about your recovery," I said.

He confided in me that it had been a twelve-year journey battling addiction, drug use, and bi-polar disorder. He had been sober forty-five days for the first time since he was eighteen years old. I empathized. I know how difficult it is to overcome various strongholds, and I have supported family members who have also struggled in these areas as well. I felt moved to share my testimony and what God has done in my life. I could see Jose's face brighten up as I shared words of encouragement with Him. When we arrived at the security checkpoint, we both pulled out our boarding passes.

"What gate are you flying out of?" I asked.

"Gate D3," Jose said.

I looked at my boarding pass. "Wow, that's the same gate as me. Are you connecting through Dallas?" I asked.

"Yes," Jose replied.

"Looks like we're on the same flight," I said. "Where are you sitting?"

"25B," he replied.

Of course he was. My assigned seat was right next to him, 25A. We both shared a look of amazement and tried to play it cool through security. At this point, I knew the Lord had orchestrated my second divine appointment of the day. I could have missed it had I been hidden behind my headphones and too preoccupied with *my agenda*.

As we headed to the terminal, I asked Jose if he had a personal relationship with God and what he knew about Jesus. I learned that his mother was Protestant and that his father was Catholic. He confessed he did not have a personal relationship with Christ and had never accepted Jesus as his Savior.

We sat together at the gate waiting for our boarding call and shared what the Lord had done in both of our lives and how His faithfulness had rescued us from the path that was leading to death and self-destruction. Right then and there, I asked Jose if I could pray for him before the flight took off. He agreed. I reached over, took his hand, and began praying for healing over his body and deliverance from addiction. I prayed against any temptation that would lead him back down the wrong path.

Friends lead friends to Jesus. In the middle of the prayer, I asked Jose if he desired to accept Jesus Christ as his Lord and Savior. "Yes," he said with a look of freedom in his eyes. He followed my lead and echoed a salvation prayer and accepted Jesus in concourse D of the Fort Myers, Florida, airport. A calm spirit came over me. I sensed that he felt it as well. As the prayer concluded, a smile formed on both of our faces. The jitters in his hands and legs I noticed earlier slowly faded away. He rested his head back on the seat for the next half hour.

Once we boarded the plane, I introduced Jose to a friend from the conference, and together we celebrated Jose's homecoming into the kingdom of God. I could hardly believe it. Jose was a new man from the one I had met an hour earlier. His smile was wide, and his eyes were glowing. I switched seats with him so he could have the window seat. He slept for most of the flight.

I continued to pray for healing over his mind, body, and soul. I stood in the gap for Jose that day. While sitting in his seat, I prayed over him for the next two hours. I believe it was a gift and a privilege that God gave me. After we landed in Dallas, we gave each other a hug and took a photo to document the moment before we parted ways. I hope and pray that one day I will see or hear about what the Lord has done in his life. Either way, I know where Jose is headed after his days on earth are over. He has an eternal destination.

God's calling will meet your heart's desire. The weeks preceding both of my divine appointments—first with Jack and then with Jose—I had been praying that the Lord would provide me an opportunity to be His hands and feet. Many of my kingdom efforts are behind the scenes. My field work was limited at that time in my life. I had been feeling overwhelmed with administrative duties. I felt like I was getting rusty with my daily evangelism efforts. My spiritual discontent led me to a place of seeking participation. I called out to God, and it was as if God was saying, "I'm ready to bring one of my children home. I need you to show up and raise your hand. Can you do that for me?" I was reminded of the words of Isaiah:

Then I heard the voice of the Lord saying, "Whom shall I send? And who will go for us?"

And I said, "Here am I, send me!" [1]

The Lord was faithful, answering my prayer and refreshing my spirit by using me to show Jose the way back to his Father. As a servant of God, I see plenty of daily opportunities I have to openly share the gospel. But first, I need to obey His call to be still and know that He is God. [2] To follow His direction and His instructions. I could have missed my opportunity to hear Jack's testimony. I could have missed the opportunity to lead Jose to salvation. I will never forget Jose or Jack and that fateful morning when I chose to be present and to raise my hand to do God's work. Praise the Lord.

step seven

CARRY OUT YOUR MISSION

NEVER GIVE UP

START WITH YOUR HEART

"You will know them by their fruits." [1]

We achieve a healthy heart through our intimacy with God. By obeying God's will, His commands, and the laws laid forth in His Word, we strengthen the root of our fruit. If the root of your heart is healthy, the fruit of your labors will be healthy. A healthy tree produces rich, delicious, abundant fruit. The same can be said about a healthy heart. Conversely, an unhealthy heart produces fruit that may be premature, tasteless, or even spoiled.

"A good tree produces good fruit, and a bad tree produces bad fruit. A good tree can't produce bad fruit, and a bad tree can't produce good fruit. So every tree that does not produce good fruit is chopped down and thrown into the fire. Yes, just as you can identify a tree by its fruit, so you can identify people by their actions." [2]

Jesus's will is for you to bear good fruit. To bear good fruit means to lead people to Christ and disciple them properly in the ways of Jesus through His teachings. This should be every believer's mission. So how do you do that? **It starts with a desire in your heart.** That is followed up by a declaration, an agreement that you will commit your days and your schedule toward activities that result in fruit bearing.

Bearing fruit takes courage. It takes confidence and boldness to bring up Christ in conversation with everyone you meet. Over the years, I've become bolder in expressing my faith from the minute that I meet someone. I do my best to pray with every single person that I meet for the first time, whether or not they are a believer. I spend some time getting to know the individual by asking questions about their life. Then I share my testimony. I explain the power of prayer, tell them I would like to pray for them, and then lead them in prayer.

Do not be afraid to pray with strangers. The power of God's Word will not come back void. Modern-day culture is so concerned about being politically correct and not offending anyone that people tend to shy away from the everyday opportunities to introduce people to Christ. I have found that when you bring the Lord into the conversation, regardless of the faith of the individual who you're sharing with, it is a positive experience. If presented properly, the fruit of the Spirit is like a magnet that draws people in. The first impression is: did that just happen? The second impression is: I feel better than I did a few minutes ago. The third impression is: I desire more of Jesus in my life. I have experimented with this method with hundreds of people throughout my lifetime. The result is consistent. It ends with a smile. People are open to hearing about God.

I will praise you, LORD, with all my heart;
I will tell of all the marvelous things you have done. [3]

Praising the Lord wholeheartedly is easier said than done. Going to church on Sunday and singing songs of praise with friends and family in your car and at home are enjoyable. Praising God through thick and thin is another story. Praising God when your life is in the dumps or when a life circumstance happens that creates tragedy all around you is where the rubber meets the road. Praising the Lord day in and day out, rain or shine, starts with the desire in your heart.

Just as a loving parent knows what's best for a child, God knows what's best for you. Do you trust Him implicitly for your well-being? If so, regardless of what the day hands you, choose to praise Him. Even in your darkest hour, He is there. Many times, He uses life-changing events to reveal something in your life that He wants you to be aware of so that you may grow. Praising Him in these dark hours is what shows true character and your loyalty and devotion to Him. When God can see that your happiness and well-being are not attached to worldly outcomes, the trust is built between you and Him, between His heart and your heart.

To maintain that connection with Him, do not allow things into your heart that should not be there. Selfish ambition, selfish intentions, and selfish ways lead to a corrupt heart. If you stockpile a treasury of bad memories, deep childhood wounds, pain, shame, guilt, anger, despair, bitterness, or resentment, you will live a miserable life. Removing this stockpile requires a specific strategy. It takes help from others who can see past the barriers of your heart, those who are willing to walk with you on the journey to replace the stockpile of false treasure with pure and life-giving treasure from heaven.

Because of your unfailing love, I can enter your house;
I will worship at your Temple with deepest awe. [4]

Worship God's name. As you fill your heart with His treasures, you will be overcome with awe of who He is. Consider the world around you. Marvel over all that He created. Look at your own body and wonder about the magnificence of its design. These awe-inspiring moments of feeling are the depth of intimacy God seeks to draw out of you when you worship Him. The fact that you were given a mind and the ability to hear, see, touch, feel, and experience the world as you do is truly amazing in itself. The detail in His creation, the beauty in the landscape, the freshness of the air, the palette of the colors, the range of sounds, the taste of food, the warmth of a touch, the design of the divine, the unexplainable, the galaxies, the universe—even the science, math, physiology, psychology, and anthropology of it all. It's too much for any person to wrap their mind around. But the divine designer did it all in six days and rested on the seventh. He created millions of species and creatures and designed the beauty of Planet Earth. This is the God you serve.

Don't worship the creation; worship the Creator. As amazing as the creation of earth is, the fact that there is a divine being behind this beautiful creation who desires a personal relationship with you is what's more magnificent. The fact that this supreme being is accessible and can be communicated with at any moment is the silver lining of His divine design.

But let all who take refuge in you be glad;
let them ever sing for joy.
Spread your protection over them,
that those who love your name may rejoice in you. [5]

Love the name of Jesus. Blasphemy is not a common word in today's lingo. The fact that people choose to use the words God and Jesus in vain is a shame. The power of the word God, the power of the word Jesus, is encompassed by the power of love. When you use God's name in vain, you invite hate, anger, and despair in the room. When you lift up God's name, you invite love into the atmosphere. If you love God's name, if you love Jesus's name, it hurts you when others dishonor His name. You feel it in your heart and soul.

Did you ever have a good friend and heard others talking poorly about them? Or maybe a family member or a child who you deeply love and somebody said something bad about them? Your response was likely to stand up and defend that person. This is how you should feel when people slander the name of Jesus. Cherish the name of your Lord and protect it. Esteem and worship His name above all else. Speak His name boldly and defend it with honor.

Mission Principle 25
The roots in your heart determine the fruits
of your labor.

Path to Progress

Desire to praise the Lord with all of your heart. *Psalm 9:1*
Choose not to follow the path of evil people. *Proverbs 4:14*
Decide to guard your heart more than anything else. *Proverbs 4:23*
The **result** is God will grant you the desires of your heart. *Psalm 37:4*
The **promise** is your heart determines your life's path. *Proverbs 4:23*

Question from Jesus
"Did not the one who made the outside make the inside also?" [6]

Questions to Meditate On
What is God speaking into your heart this season?
What roots in your heart are a stronghold for evil?
Are your words drawing others in or pushing others away?
What are the fruits of your labor for God?

Your Call to Action
Become a magnet for Christ. Draw people in.
Refine your vocabulary. Start with your heart.

PLANT YOUR VINEYARD

"And the seeds that fell on the good soil represent honest, good-hearted people who hear God's word, cling to it, and patiently produce a huge harvest." [1]

To find purpose is to find joy and fulfillment. Living out God's purpose for your life is the secret to the intimacy you desire with Him. When you are living a kingdom lifestyle, in constant communication with the Lord, your heart is full, your smile is wide, and your impact on others runs deep. Jesus used the metaphor of planting and tending to a vineyard throughout Scripture when describing the kingdom of heaven. By planting a vineyard with Christ and tending to that vineyard, you will unlock an ongoing life of joy and fulfillment.

That person is like a tree planted by streams of water,
which yields its fruit in season
and whose leaf does not wither—
whatever they do prospers. [2]

It takes the written *and* spoken Word of God to bear much fruit. God gave you His Word so you could read it and store it within your heart, but He also wants you to speak it. When you speak God's Word, you breathe life into the world around you. The result is that you're sowing seeds into the hearts of those who hear it. Those seeds grow little by little into vineyards of their own. That fruit bears more fruit and produces more seed, in turn bearing more fruit.

God's plan for multiplication using His Word is quite a phenomenon. Seeds of life sprout by humans simply communicating His Word to one another, resulting in growth, healing, and blessings. All this from a single source of living water inside the pages of the Bible. Like a sponge absorbing water, sometimes you need to be squeezed to let God's holy living water out of you by pouring into others. Then you can go back to the well to soak up more living water. Discover God's divine design. You will never thirst for anything else. *"But whoever drinks the water I give them will never thirst. Indeed, the water I give them will become in them a spring of water welling up to eternal life."* [3]

God has you here on earth for a reason. His plan will decide how long you need to be here to carry out your mission. He also gives you free will. With free will comes the right to make choices and decisions. If we freely choose and decide not to evangelize, not to obey, not to bear fruit, why are we surprised when we have affliction in our lives?

"You are the salt of the earth. But if the salt loses its saltiness, how can it be made salty again? It is no longer good for anything, except to be thrown out and trampled underfoot." [4] *"He cuts off every branch of mine that doesn't produce fruit, and he prunes the branches that do bear fruit so they will produce even more."* [5]

You will rarely hear these verses from the pulpit. They're some of those "hush-hush" verses that most pastors and priests avoid. The bottom line is: If you lose your flavor or don't bear fruit, you're actually worthless to the vineyard and to the branch. You are cut off. If a flower is wilting, you see it needs water, so you water it. But if a flower doesn't open up, you simply throw it away. It's a kingdom of heaven principle. It may sound harsh, but it's the truth. We don't get to make up the guidelines; we are subject to them. You and I were built to labor for God. *"The harvest is great, but the workers are few."* [6]

The fact is that most people don't have an exemplary work ethic. Most people align with the saying, "Less work, more play." Yet, our Maker designed us to create, build, design, and labor. Yes, rest is a necessity, but God did not design you to be idle for long periods of time. You were designed to progress, advance, grow, and thrive. For many, this is the main battleground inside the heart: the work it takes to fulfill God's will versus the temptation of fulfilling your own. Which side is winning the battle inside your heart?

May the favor of the Lord our God rest on us;
establish the work of our hands for us—
yes, establish the work of our hands. [7]

Even if it is more work, build your house on solid rock. This ensures that it stands rock solid when the storms of life surge your way. The same could be said when it's time to plant your vineyard. You need to plant on healthy soil. That soil is cultivated in your heart. If you plan to bear much fruit for the kingdom, the soil needs to be rich with nutrients and able to be tilled so the plants grow deep roots. Just like the house is not shaken by the winds of a storm, your vineyard will not be uprooted by heavy winds that bring difficulty and persecution. Stand on solid ground and praise the Lord through thick and thin. It is He who is capable of protecting the vineyard. He has a vested interest in watching that your plants bear much fruit.

Now I stand on solid ground,
and I will publicly praise the LORD. [8]

Expect persecution as you journey into the mission field. The mission field can be right outside your front door. When others give you objections or flat out reject your faith and conviction in Christ, you are sharpening your two-edged sword. Rejection prepares and strengthens you to be an overcomer. Learn to deflect those objections by reading God's Word, and remember that persecution builds character.

"Since they persecuted me, naturally they will persecute you." [8]

As you set off on your mission, be prepared to be turned away, met with disdain, ridiculed, laughed at, and mocked. You will be tempted to retreat to your circle of influence where it's safe and comfortable. It's easy being around people who share your values, morals, ethics, and political views. If you retreat, the enemy has won the battle. If this happens on a recurring basis, the fruit that God planned for your life will dwindle from much fruit to little fruit.

Don't be surprised at the fiery trials you are going through, as if something strange were happening to you. Instead, be very glad—for these trials make you partners with Christ in his suffering, so that you will have the wonderful joy of seeing his glory when it is revealed to all the world. [9]

Fair-weather Christians do not last long. When trials show up in their lives, they quake. If you're going to follow Christ, plan on being persecuted and antagonized. Your response to that antagonizing person or persecutor is what separates you as a follower of Christ from the rest of the world. It's not you who are responding but the Holy Spirit within you. By exercising the fruit of the Spirit, you can respond the same way Jesus would respond.

And while He was being accused by the chief priests and elders, He answered nothing.

Then Pilate said to Him, "Do You not hear how many things they testify against You?" But He answered him not one word, so that the governor marveled greatly. [11]

Before Jesus was killed, He was blamed for many things that He did not do. He was lied about, beaten, then crucified for crimes He did not commit. Yet He remained silent. Why? Obedience to doing His Father's will. In His darkest hour, Jesus showed His devotion and loyalty to God. He knew the excruciating pain that awaited Him, yet He submitted to His Father's plan. *"Father, if you are willing, please take this cup of suffering away from me. Yet I want your will to be done, not mine."* [12]

Your moment of truth is coming. Everyone has their moment of truth during their lifetime. Many people have multiple moments that are often referred to as *defining* moments. For Jesus, His defining moment was when He stood before Pontius Pilate. His accusers lied and slandered Him and yet He remained silent. If Jesus had allowed idols or roadblocks into His heart, He would not have been able to love God with *all* of His heart in His moment of truth. When your moment comes, will you be able to love God with all of your heart?

Wait patiently for the LORD.
Be brave and courageous.
Yes, wait patiently for the LORD. [13]

God calls you to live courageously. Be brave. As you expand your territory, resistance will come your way. Adverse climates will arise, and thieves will try to steal your crop. Weeds will try to choke your plants. When these seasons arrive, this is the time for you to be brave and courageous. Stand up and take control of your vineyard. Remember you were appointed to *administer* the harvest. You are not *responsible* for the harvest. That is God's job. The Holy Spirit will bring the harvest to fruition. Christ will be there with you. Your job is to help God prune and protect the vineyard. Your job is to gather laborers to send into the field to help you with His harvest. Seek brave and courageous workers for your field, workers who are willing to endure the tough climates. How do you get started? Plant the first seed. Share your testimony with someone today.

Mission Principle 26
Turn your vineyard into a bountiful harvest for
Christ's kingdom.

Day 26

Path to Progress

Desire to be courageous and brave. *Psalm 27:14*
Choose to take a stand and praise God in public. *Psalm 26:12*
Decide to tell others about God's wonders and all the things He has done. *Psalm 22:30-31*
The **result** is stories of His faithfulness will be passed on to future generations. *Psalm 22:31*
The **promise** is the entire world will acknowledge God. *Psalm 22:27*

Question from Jesus
"Do you believe that I am able to do this?" [14]

Questions to Meditate On
Do you consider yourself a laborer of God?
Do you see fruit in your life from your heavenly vineyard?
Is God's harvest a priority in your life?
What is preventing you from yielding a plentiful harvest?

Your Call to Action
Obey God. Plant your vineyard.
Sow seeds. Grow and harvest.

Day 27

SUBMIT TO A KINGDOM SCHEDULE

"My nourishment comes from doing the will of God, who sent me, and from finishing his work." [1]

To effectively carry out God's will, you will need to reprioritize your days. Your new schedule will reflect a kingdom calendar with kingdom-focused activities as you embark on a kingdom lifestyle. Your two main priorities will be: (1) developing your Christ-like character and (2) carrying out God's will. You will move from a *salvation relationship* with Christ to a life of *full surrender* with your eternal Father and His son, Jesus Christ. His priorities will become yours. The things of this world will become less important and less relevant. They will cease to affect your well-being and happiness.

Devote yourself to a Christ-centered schedule. You have the opportunity to interact with Jesus Himself by following His commands. While here on earth, He told us six ways to interact with Him on a daily basis.

"'For I was hungry and you gave me something to eat (1), I was thirsty and you gave me something to drink (2), I was a stranger and you invited me in (3), I needed clothes and you clothed me (4), I was sick and you looked after me (5), I was in prison and you came to visit me (6).'" [2]

Jesus said that when you do these for others, you are actually doing these things unto Him. *"Truly I tell you, whatever you did for one of the least of these brothers and sisters of mine, you did for me."* [3] Jesus also said that when you refuse to help those in need, you, in turn, refuse to help Jesus. *"'For I was hungry and you gave me nothing to eat, I was thirsty and you gave me nothing to drink.'"* [4]

We can express our gratitude and thankfulness to Jesus while carrying out His will in many ways. Feeding the hungry or getting involved in clean water initiatives, clothing drives, helping strangers, medical volunteering, and visiting those who are incarcerated are just a few. We have the opportunity here on earth to love each other the same way God loves us, through provisions and care.

We often miss these opportunities because of pure laziness or blame shift. Within my real estate company, I teach real estate agents to avoid both of these deterrents. Over the years, I consistently heard the same excuses why real estate agents were unable to achieve success. They would shift the blame to something or someone else as the reason why they could not move forward in prospecting or successfully carrying out sales in their business. I finally made a blame shift list for agents to avoid as part of my *Mastering Your B.S.* training series. The B.S. stands for **behavior** and **skills**. It also stands for **blame shift**. The blame shift list can be applied to carrying out God's will as well. Here are the most popular excuses why someone refuses to carry out God's will:

I don't have enough time …
I'm too busy with my job or family …
As soon as I …
This month … this year … this season …
It's my church …
This person is holding me back … (choose your favorite family member)

Then you will show discernment,
and your lips will express what you've learned. [5]

Avoid blame shift by choosing discernment. Wisdom gives you the ability to discern the right choice and make the right decision. Where does that discernment come from? The Holy Spirit gives you the ability to discern by asking Him what to do. Did you ask Him? If you're operating independently and making your own choices and decisions, the results are 50/50 at best. When you consult the Holy Spirit, listen, and reference the Word of God for validation, you increase your probability of making the right decision. Ask the Holy Spirit to show you discernment through a word, a sign, or a validation through somebody who you trust. Patience and listening are the keys with discernment.

For His anger is but for a moment,
His favor is for life;
Weeping may endure for a night,
But joy comes in the morning. [6]

When you submit to a kingdom schedule, you are signing up for God's direction for a lifetime. The fear of being *controlled* by a calendar starts to fade away. Once you realize that your calendar provides the necessary structure for you to follow God's commands, a wonderful feeling of relief sinks in. It's now on autopilot. Seek the Holy Spirit for guidance on how to organize your days.

Put God first. Structure your day to begin by praising God. Spend time with Him each morning through prayer, and listen for His voice as you read His Word. Your one on one time should precede the rest of your day. After breakfast, spend time prospecting. Prospecting means actively seeking out those who do not have a relationship with Christ. Who are your prospects for the day? This can be done anywhere you go. It could be at work; it could be in your neighborhood; it can be done anywhere God leads you. Take your freshest energy during the early hours of the day, usually before noon, and prospect. Do the one thing that will yield the most fruit for His vineyard. Break for lunch, take a break and enjoy the afternoon. When you catch your second wind, continue prospecting or disciple someone who is growing in Christ. This is a kingdom schedule in action.

Whatever God has for you today, do it with all of your might. Spend time with your family, your loved ones, and your children as the day starts to unwind. Remember to break bread and spend time praying with your loved ones. Prepare to sleep by reading more of God's Word.

Reflect back on the day, looking at the things that worked and at things that didn't work. Make your plans for tomorrow. Stay focused on your schedule and on His will.

Consult with God throughout the day. Ask Him if He has suggestions on how you can improve your performance. Just like a great student goes to the teacher to ask for suggestions, you can go to Him and ask for approval of your daily activities. He will help you. This is a healthy relationship; this is *normal*. As your day winds down, prepare to rest soundly and peacefully by filling your mind with healthy inputs and substances that honor God. Whether that's spending time in the Bible, with family members, watching a positive and uplifting movie, playing a game, reading a book, talking a walk, socializing with friends, or any other healthy activity as long as it honors God. The goal is to draw the day to a close in a healthy mind-set. This way, your mind and body are prepared to rest well. God will fill up the chambers of your heart with joy, energy, and enthusiasm so you are ready for the next day.

By sticking to your schedule throughout the week, you will be able to rest on the Sabbath as the Lord intended. It was made to rest and recover. The Sabbath was not designed to be the one day of the week when you try to fit in God and then jump right back into your busy routine that ends up draining your tank. That kind of lifestyle leads to disease and many other forms of mental, physical, and emotional distress.

But as for me, I trust in You, O LORD;
I say, "You are my God." [7]

Learn to take an employee mind-set. Make the firm decision that the Lord *is* your God. He is your boss and your leader. The one you are following and whose commandments you obey. As a good employee, you call your boss daily and ask, "What do you want me to do today?" Confirm with your boss before you make any big decisions to make sure the decision is what is best for the company, God's business. If you're still battling Jesus for the throne, trying to be your own god or boss, you are taking a position that Jesus is there to *serve you* rather than you being there to *serve Him*. You will constantly run into a wall with that frame of mind because, ultimately, you know that He is the boss. The mind-set of a rebellious employee is "I'm going to do what I want; I hope I don't get caught." This is a very dangerous way to think while working for God's business. It doesn't fit into a kingdom schedule. It will only result in you delaying your destiny.

The quicker you yield your schedule to Jesus's authority, the faster He can accelerate the blessing and favor in your life. It starts with the decision that *the Lord Jesus* is your God. Remove idols or anything else battling for the number one position in your life. Your top priority should not be your spouse, family, friends, hobbies, career, bank account, travel plans, sports teams, or anything else that contends for the number one spot.

Your number one is God. Once the boss says that work is done for the day, go enjoy your afternoon, evening, or weekend with your spouse, family, friends, or hobbies. There's plenty of vacation time at God's business. There's plenty of rest, relaxation, and perks reserved for *after* you serve God.

Mission Principle 27
Focus your energy on completing kingdom activities.

PATH TO PROGRESS

Desire God to guide you on the correct path. *Psalm 23:3*
Choose to remain on that path. *Proverbs 4:26*
Decide that the Lord is your God. *Psalm 31:14*
The **result** is He will show you the proper path if you go astray.
Psalm 25:8
The **promise** is God is good and His actions are right. *Psalm 25:8*

Question from Jesus
*"What shall we say the kingdom of God is like, or what parable shall we use
to describe it?"* [8]

Questions to Meditate On
What do you imagine the kingdom of heaven is like?
What are your priorities?
Do those priorities honor God?
Are your priorities kingdom focused?

Your Call to Action
Document your behavioral patterns. List your priorities.
Rearrange your calendar. Submit to a kingdom schedule.

LIVE A KINGDOM LIFESTYLE

"Obedience is better than sacrifice." [1]

Living a kingdom lifestyle keeps the endgame in sight. Living a kingdom lifestyle provides immense freedom to live the way God intended you to live: a life completely dependent on Him. Through moment-to-moment interaction and seeking His direction for wisdom, knowledge, and understanding for any choice or decision, you are operating in the same manner that Jesus did when He was here on earth. Jesus woke up early, spent time with His Father, communicated His daily plans, and listened to what His Father told Him to do.

He guards the paths of justice,
And preserves the way of His saints. [2]

How do you develop a kingdom lifestyle? Developing a kingdom-focused mind-set requires you to create a lifestyle in which you are reminded of the truth over and over again, just as Jesus consistently reminded His disciples of the truth. Total submission to a kingdom lifestyle requires complete trust that God has your back. He will guard your path and protect you when you are faithful to Him. *Love the LORD, all you godly ones! / For the LORD protects those who are loyal to him, / but he harshly punishes the arrogant.* [3]

"Blessed are those who hunger and thirst for righteousness,
For they shall be filled." [4]

When you live a kingdom lifestyle, you live with heaven in mind. Imagine waking up every morning not having to worry about your needs or what you will eat. Imagine not having to fear what evil might be done toward you today or dwelling on something that somebody said that was hurtful. Imagine being carefree and eradicating all unrighteousness that bothers you, leaves you restless, and affects your sleep or physical well-being. This is what the kingdom of God is like. And it's your inheritance.

Nurture your relationship with the Holy Spirit. The Holy Spirit needs access to your mind, body, and soul. He will help you make wise decisions on a moment-by-moment basis. You will learn to seek the Holy Spirit's counsel on every aspect of your life. You will be referencing God's Word to validate that what you are hearing is accurate. A kingdom lifestyle starts with praising God and putting Him at the front and center of your day. It continues by seeking out God's will for that day, whatever He would have you do. Have you asked Him what He desires from you today?

Throughout the day, you will be loving others and changing their lives by blessing them as Christ did to those around Him. Regardless of who you run into, rich or poor, you're treating each person equally. Meanwhile, God is lining up divine appointments for you as you're completing His mission every single day. As you go from assignment to assignment, your life becomes one of glory to glory, from one accomplishment for God to the next. You pause, celebrate for a moment, catch your breath, and carry on.

But we all, with unveiled face, beholding as in a mirror the glory of the Lord, are being transformed into the same image from glory to glory, just as by the Spirit of the Lord. [5]

As each day winds down, you spend time with your heavenly Father. You rejoice with your family members, recounting all the things that He did with you that day. You move forward to a night of sleep dreaming about all of the things that God will do with you tomorrow. He shares dreams with you about the vision that He has for your life in the foreseeable future. Your heart prompts this question in your mind: How can I help my heavenly Father till the land, build the vineyard, and bring in the harvest? Your lifestyle includes teaching and discipling others how to live that lifestyle.

A kingdom lifestyle includes placing Christ at the center of your marriage. By aligning your marriage with God's will, you set a model example for your children and grandchildren of how to fulfill God's will as a family unit, not a lone ranger.

Encourage your entire extended family to participate so all facets of your family's next generation will continue to fulfill God's will. "All hands on deck" is a great phrase to describe how God designed the family unit to complete God's missions together. Once the entire family is in motion, completing missions, this pattern will pass from generation to generation, resulting in a kingdom legacy.

Jesus illustrated what a kingdom lifestyle looks like while here on earth. He taught us about the Holy Spirit and how to engage God's Spirit in our lives.

+ "He [the Holy Spirit] will guide you into all truth." [6]
+ "He [the Holy Spirit] will tell you about the future." [7]
+ "He [the Holy Spirit] will teach you everything." [8]
+ "[The Holy Spirit] will remind you of everything I [Jesus] have told you." [9]
+ "The Holy Spirit gives birth to spiritual life." [10]
+ "He is the Holy Spirit ... he lives with you now and later will be in you." [11]
+ "He [the Holy Spirit] will not speak on His own authority, but whatever He hears He will speak." [12]
+ "He [the Holy Spirit] will convict the world of its sin, and of God's righteousness, and of the coming judgment." [13]
+ "The Spirit will tell you whatever he receives from me [Jesus]." [14]
+ "God is Spirit, so those who worship him must worship in spirit and truth." [15]

+ *"No one can enter the Kingdom of God without being born of water and the Spirit."* [16]

There's another important way to engage in a kingdom lifestyle after inviting the Holy Spirit in.

Tie them on your fingers as a reminder.
Write them [God's commands] deep within your heart. [17]

Write God's instructions deep into your heart so that you never forget them. Some people are able to do this by memorizing Bible verses so that they can recount those Bible verses when the need arises. The Holy Spirit will bring those words and verses to mind when you need them most. Part of a kingdom lifestyle is to meditate on God's Word throughout the day so you can recall it at any time.

Preach the word; be prepared in season and out of season; correct, rebuke and encourage—with great patience and careful instruction. [18]

You don't know the circumstances or life questions that today will present, but you can prepare by storing God's Word, which has all the answers, deep into your heart. At any given moment, you can be presented with a handful of challenges of various natures. By storing all of His answers and holy wisdom in your heart, you will be ready in season and out of season with an answer for any question that comes up. Learn to live a kingdom lifestyle.

Mission Principle 28
Living a kingdom lifestyle is necessary to fulfill God's will.

Day 28

PATH TO PROGRESS

Desire to live in God's house forever. *Psalm 23:6*
Choose to write God's instructions deep inside your heart. *Proverbs 7:3*
Decide to lead a life without blame and act justly. *Psalm 15:2*
The **result** is you will be able to stand firm forever. *Psalm 15:5*
The **promise** is God will guard your path if you're just; He will protect you if you are faithful to Him. *Proverbs 2:8*

Question from Jesus
"Do you bring in a lamp to put it under a bowl or a bed? Instead, don't you put it on its stand?" [19]

Questions to Meditate On
Are you pursuing a worldly lifestyle or a heavenly lifestyle?
What is your time most devoted to?
Why do you do what you do?
Who is the boss of your life?

Your Call to Action
Analyze your life. Engage the Spirit.
Memorize Scripture. Live a kingdom lifestyle.

Day 29

START FISHING TODAY

"Come, follow me, and I will show you how to fish for people!" [1]

Leading others to Christ requires prospecting. Prospecting is actively seeking out those who do not have a relationship with Christ. All prospecting activities involve some form of doubt, fear, and rejection. In the business world, the one thing no one wants to do on a daily basis is prospecting. Why is that? Because it's a task that requires overcoming objections. Prospecting has no tolerance for laziness or procrastination. However, prospecting is the key to any business growth and long-term success. The same is true for spiritual growth when spreading the good news.

Learn to fish. Jesus gave you instructions on how to bring people to the saving knowledge of Jesus Christ in the Scriptures. As your leader, He will teach you His methods to become an exceptional fisherman. While on earth, He used a fishing pole, bait, and a hook. The fishing pole Jesus used was His human body, an extension of God the Father. For bait, Jesus used the signs and wonders manifested through His godly character. The hook that Jesus used was the Word of God. The transformation in people's lives on the spot was undeniably divine. Following His example, you have the ability to model His methods on a daily basis. He gave you the Holy Spirit to help you fish.

"The Holy Spirit, whom the Father will send in my name, will teach you all things and will remind you of everything I have said to you." [2]

You have received wisdom from the heavens above. You have been given the truth, a path, and a light to guide your way. You're excited. Excited to share Jesus with the world, you set off on your mission to make disciples, share the gospel, and bring people to Christ. But then life gets in the way. The pep in your step may carry you through your late teenage years and into your early twenties, but little by little, life gets in the way. You start a family and your children are young; they need you. Your spouse needs you; your work needs you; your church needs you. There are so many things to keep you *busy being busy*, distracting you from your mission. Bringing the kingdom of heaven here to earth is your purpose. Stay focused and do not be discouraged. The harvest is ripe.

Learn to adapt. When Jesus walked this earth, He had the ability to be a chameleon. He could sit next to a poor woman and look her in the eye with love, touch a blind man and heal him; then later that evening, He could sit next to a rich man and convict him of his folly. You have the same ability through the Holy Spirit. Jesus said in His Scripture: *"Whoever has ears, let them hear."* [3] Your responsibility is to speak up; the Word of God does the rest. When you stay silent, the Word is dormant in your body and your branches are unfruitful.

God is worthy of your honor. Choose to broadcast God's faithfulness, His unfailing love, and His saving power to everybody you know. There's nothing more glorifying to your Maker than sharing with others what He has done in your life. If you want to honor God, share with others what He has done and is doing in your life today.

I do not hide your righteousness in my heart;
I speak of your faithfulness and your saving help.
I do not conceal your love and your faithfulness
from the great assembly. [4]

The Word of God was meant to be openly shared. *"Whoever has ears, let them hear."* [5] God will draw in those who are listening, those whose eyes are open, and those whose hearts are prepared to change. Your job is to be vocal, bold, and courageous. Speak directly using point-blank vocabulary with kind, compassionate words that draw people in, not push them away.

"If they had listened to me, they would listen to you." [6]

Learn to dismantle walls. Jesus will teach you to reveal the walls in people's hearts. The walls that get built around people's hearts are what prevent them from submitting and having a relationship with Christ. A heart transformation needs to take place within them to accept Christ as their Savior. Sharing with others how God transformed your life by growing your wisdom and knowledge of how to operate here on earth is a great storyline to lead others to a heart transformation of their own. Sharing how God has changed your life will draw people in rather than push them away. When you focus your attention on the hearts of others and explore the wounds and bruises from their past, you may be met with pushback, rejection, and anger triggered by pain that usually shuts someone down. Think carefully about how you present who Jesus is to others. Your best testimony is reflected by your character and your lifestyle.

Sing praises to the LORD who reigns in Jerusalem.
Tell the world about his unforgettable deeds. [7]

God is a storyteller. He chose to communicate His Word through stories about individuals throughout history in the Bible. He wants you to write your story with Him. If you feel your story is uninteresting or yet to be developed, this is something to seek God about. The question is: What is holding you back from writing the script of your life?

God loves stories. There's no better way to bring God glory than by telling your story. Each one of us has a story, and a beautiful one at that. There is no better testimony than sharing a great story about what God has done in your life with someone who is learning about God. If you are serving God and walking with Him *on a daily basis,* then you should have enough stories to fill books upon books. If you're not documenting all the magnificent things God does in your life, it's time to begin today. This way you will be prepared when someone asks. You can simply pull out your journal and start to recount all the amazing things that God has done. If you have a prayer journal, turn it into a praise journal. Then turn your praise journal into a story journal.

If you truly seek God's will, He will lay out the adventure of a lifetime. This gives you a platform to glorify Him by sharing that adventure with others as it's unfolding. At some point in your life, you've had something happen where it was clear it was no coincidence. Everything lined up just in the nick of time for you to be able to move forward. A friend of mine, Brad Formsma, and I often reflect about God's incredible goodness in our lives by saying to each other, "You can't write this stuff." Meaning, if you tried to sit down and write out or imagine the stories God plans to be a part of your life, there is no way you could document His timing and orchestration that seem to line up in an inexplicable way.

"Everyone who acknowledges me [Jesus] publicly here on earth, the Son of Man will also acknowledge in the presence of God's angels." [8]

Acknowledging Jesus in public is so much fun. When He's presented properly, watching the expression of others light up when you talk about God is amazing. When you boldly and confidently speak about a God you know intimately who blesses you, loves you, and looks after you, it's infectious. Everyone seeks a heavenly Father. You were designed to seek Him. To deny Him is to deny your own well-being.

Jesus gives you clear instructions to share His message to others.
+ *"Go into all the world and preach the Good News to everyone."* [9]
+ *"As you go, proclaim this message: 'The kingdom of heaven has come near.'"* [10]
+ *"Go and make disciples of all the nations, baptizing them in the name of the Father and the Son and the Holy Spirit."* [11]

When sharing the gospel with others, it can be tempting to judge another person's life. Remember, you are not the judge; God is. This is a liberating feeling. It allows you to focus on catching fish and not be overly concerned about what type of fish you catch. Leave that to God. Your job is to get on the boat, get out there, cast the net wide, and bring in fish. God in His righteousness will deal with each person one on one.

Many people feel unworthy of God's love. They may feel as though their sin is too great for God's forgiveness. Your job is to share with them that no matter what they've done in their lives, or how much guilt and shame they may or may not feel, your God is a God of mercy and forgiveness. No sin is too great for God to forgive except speaking against the Holy Spirit.

"And so I tell you, every kind of sin and slander can be forgiven, but blasphemy against the Spirit will not be forgiven. Anyone who speaks a word against the Son of Man will be forgiven, but anyone who speaks against the Holy Spirit will not be forgiven, either in this age or in the age to come." [12]

You can display grace and mercy toward someone you are leading to Christ by sharing stories of God's goodness in your life, opening up and being vulnerable, and confiding in that person the shame and guilt that you felt previously before you had a relationship with a righteous God, a God who forgives you. The open-hearted evangelism will draw the attention of others who are living in sin and in pain. Your transparency will translate to saving lives.

Sharing your testimony allows healing in your heart. When you open up and accept the reality of your sin and discuss how God forgave you and, in turn, showed you how to overcome it, others are inspired to follow your lead. By illuminating the right path, an additional benefit for you kicks in, which allows a type of intimate redemptive forgiveness through reconciliation between you and God. By expressing God's unfailing love to others, you are able to move forward in your own life. By openly addressing your sin, it will help others to learn from it and at the same time help you to let go of it, allowing you to rejoice in God's forgiveness.

*He will judge the world with justice
and rule the nations with fairness.*

The LORD is a shelter for the oppressed,
a refuge in times of trouble. [13]

Remember that love never fails. God is love, so therefore, God can never fail. He has the power to save you and to save others through you. Who can you lead to Him today?

Mission Principle 29
The greatest return on investment is a human
soul turning to Jesus.

Day 29

Path to Progress

Desire to proclaim His name in front of others. *Psalm 22:22*
Choose to tell others all of the marvelous and unforgettable things God
has done in your life. *Psalm 9:1, 11*
Decide to praise God. *Psalm 22:22, 25*
The **result** is God will judge in your favor, have mercy on you,
and be a refuge when you're in trouble. *Psalm 9:8-9*
The **promise** is if you trust in God, you will never be disgraced.
Psalm 22:5

Question from Jesus
"Friends, haven't you any fish?" [14]

Questions to Meditate On
Are you openly sharing your faith with others?
Is prospecting a daily habit?
How often do you share your testimony?
Is fear of rejection preventing you from fishing?

Your Call to Action
Acknowledge Jesus. Share your testimony.
Learn to prospect. Start fishing today.

Day 30

RESPOND TO YOUR MAKER

"Not everyone who calls out to me, 'Lord! Lord!' will enter the Kingdom of Heaven. Only those who actually do the will of my Father in heaven will enter. On judgment day many will say to me, 'Lord! Lord! We prophesied in your name and cast out demons in your name and performed many miracles in your name.' But I will reply, 'I never knew you. Get away from me, you who break God's laws.'" [1]

How important is fulfilling God's will for your life? This is life's most important matter at hand. Your salvation, eternal life, and entrance into heaven depend on it. If you ask any Christian if they are going to be turned away on judgment day by Christ Himself, they will say, "No way. I'm saved by grace. I said the salvation prayer. I go to church on Christmas *and* Easter. I am definitely going to heaven." If you read the verse above carefully, there is a condition, and the condition is: **"Only those who actually do the will of my Father will enter."**

What Christ is saying is that by following God's commandments, obeying God's laws, and carrying out His will, you will be granted an entrance ticket into heaven. He is also saying that the performance and displaying of spiritual gifts or miracles is not necessarily an indication of salvation nor confirmation of being a true disciple of Christ.

Is God's grace or obedience to His Word the key to unlock heaven's door? They both are. Straying away from God's commandments and laws comes down to one word: disobedience. Every believer in Jesus has a choice. If you know His commands, then you must choose to obey, disobey, or ignore His commands. If you choose to disobey or ignore Him, you actually don't *know Him*. You know *of* Him.

The enemy's strategy to derail you from God's will is simple: distract you and deceive you into believing you are a "good person." The modern-day person's schedule is jam-packed with attention-demanding inputs requesting your presence and focus. With so many inputs draining your energy, the output suffers. The fruit of your tree suffers. Remember, the enemy is out to kill, *steal*, and destroy. By stealing your most valuable commodity, which is time, he is able to lie to you, make you believe there is not enough time in your day to carry out God's will, and, in turn, destroy the destiny God planned for your life.

I assure you, from personal experience, that once you discover your true mission—not your will, but God's will—your life will take on new meaning. Your daily lifestyle will be aligned with what you were designed to do and with who you were designed to be. Your burdens, fears, and worries will fade. The aftereffects of successfully carrying out your mission will be the love, hope, peace, and joy you desire. Contentment rests in the completion of a job well done. Jesus brought glory to God on earth **by carrying out His will.** He **completed the work** God gave Him to do. [2]

All true believers in Christ have a deep desire to bring God glory here on earth. We are able to do this by carrying out His will, overcoming adversity, and bringing God glory. When Christ was here on earth, He brought glory to God by completing the work that God gave Him to do, by carrying out His will. The key word is *completion*. Ignoring your mission, aborting your mission, or giving up halfway through is not fulfilling God's will for your life. Finishing the race, completing the mission, and staying steadfast and consistent are the keys. Jesus will light your path, guide your way, and be with you always.

God is seeking complete devotion from you. He is seeking your worship. He wants you to seek Him above all else. The number one commandment Jesus gave you while He was here on earth was to love your God with all of your heart, all of your soul, and all of your mind. God wants you to trust Him completely.

Here are seven ways God instructs you to be devoted to Him:

- Love Him with all your heart, soul, and mind. [3]
- Worship God in spirit and in truth. [4]
- Seek God's kingdom and He will provide for you. [5]
- Believe in God. Believe in Jesus. [6]
- Remain in His love. [7]
- Hate everyone in comparison to Him. [8]

Jesus addressed our devotion and loyalty to Him in these three key Scriptures:

- *"If you refuse to take up your cross and follow me [Jesus], you are not worthy of being mine."* [9]
- *"If you love your father or mother more than you love me, you are not worthy of being mine; or if you love your son or daughter more than me, you are not worthy of being mine."* [10]
- *"No one can serve two masters. For you will hate one and love the other; you will be devoted to one and despise the other."* [11]

God's instructions are simple. Love Him with all of your heart. Love your neighbor. Go make disciples. You were strategically placed here for a reason. All of your life experiences have been cultivated for such a time as this. Once you identify your mission, your purpose will be revealed.

Understanding your responsibility to your Maker and following His commands are essential elements to completing your mission in life. My hope and prayer is that this book would encourage and inspire you to know Jesus in a deeper way. Remember that no literature can ever over-shadow the actual Word of God. Read it regularly. Rest assured it will lead you down the right path to carry out God's will that He specifically designed just for you. Your mission, should you choose to accept it, is to find God's will for your life and then do it.

May God bless you on your journey,

Andrew Michael Arroyo

Mission Principle 30
Find and fulfill your responsibility to your Maker.

Day 30

PATH TO PROGRESS

Desire to give your life to the Lord. *Psalm 25:1*
Choose to talk about God's faithfulness, His power to save, and His
unfailing love. *Psalm 40:10*
Decide to delight in God's laws. *Psalm 1:2*
The **result** is God will prosper you in everything you do. *Psalm 1:3*
The **promise** is God will show you the way of life. *Psalm 16:11*

Question from Jesus

"When the Son of Man comes, will he find faith on the earth?" [12]

Questions to Meditate On

Have you responded to God's calling?
In what ways have you succeeded in fulfilling God's will?
In what ways have you failed to fulfill God's will?
What changes are you prepared to make today?

Your Call to Action

Start today. Make the changes.
Respond to your Maker. Sign the covenant. Fulfill God's will.

Part II

SUMMARY: HOW TO FULFILL GOD'S WILL

You *ignite your desire for justice* by telling God you're ready to fulfill His will. You read the Bible to *discover God's divine design*. You learn that you were created to love—and to fulfill your lifelong mission of loving God and loving others. You begin to *filter out the noise in your life* so your mind can pay attention to what is pure and true. You *accept God's promises* for what they are and don't try to modify them in the slightest. You shed all of your doubt and unbelief. Slowly, you *identify your heart's treasure* using God's divine knowledge in the Bible. You allow it to go deep into your spirit so that you gain human understanding.

You start to *cleanse your heart and mind* by removing things that don't belong there. You show God the places in your heart that need His divine healing. Little by little, God starts to operate to mend your heart. Meanwhile, you continue to *absorb God's Word* and His precious promises. During the process of absorbing God's Word, you start to *reshape your mind* and *redefine your life*. You discover your purpose in life. You realize what you were created to do. You have a fresh mind-set. You witness the life-giving power of the Holy Spirit breathing through you. You learn that you can impart that gift to others. This allows you to *choose the right path*.

Using God's wisdom, you decide to *repurpose your pursuit* in life. You choose to repave your path, so that you can embrace the blessings that God has in store for you. You *rearrange your prayer life*. Instead of asking God to fulfill your requests, you start to ask Him how you can fulfill His. You focus on fulfilling His will rather than your own will. You let go of your selfish desires. You are now empowered to *calibrate your decisions with wisdom*. It's time for you to *reveal radical results*, just like Jesus.

The journey to carry out God's will *starts in your heart*. You choose to follow Jesus's instructions and *plant your vineyard*, studying God's Word every step of the way. You *submit to a kingdom schedule* and make a commitment to *live a kingdom lifestyle*. Jesus is now the ruler of your heart, mind, and soul. His Holy Spirit encourages you to *start fishing today*. You make the wise decision to *respond to your Maker* and successfully fulfill God's will. Enjoy the journey.

LIFELONG COVENANT

Father God, I hereby express my desire to fulfill **your** will for my life.

Holy Spirit, guide me toward the right path. Give me the clarity, confidence, and wisdom to make the right decisions.

Jesus, reveal your character to me. Show me how to apply **your** likeness to my life.

I am ready to obey you and carry out my mission here on earth. Let the eternal journey begin …

Reader's Signature:

_____

Accountability Partner #1 Signature:

_____

Accountability Partner #2 Signature:

_____

Location & Date:

_____

The world and its desires pass away, but whoever does the will of God lives forever. — 1 John 2:17 (NIV)

MISSION PRINCIPLES TO FULFILL GOD'S WILL

1: Sincere faith in God is expressed by doing His will.

2: Your destiny is to become Christ-like.

3: Make God's will the primary desire of your heart.

4: Father God's business is more important than your *busyness*.

5: God's vision for your life is to establish the kingdom of heaven.

6: Shape your vision with biblical principles and values.

7: You can overcome anything when Christ is your Lord and Master.

8: The fruit of the Spirit will break the chains of spiritual bondage.

9: Follow Jesus to find God's will for your life.

10: Anything is possible with faith in God.

11: Let go. Stop wasting time on unhealthy obsessions.

12: Get your priorities straight. Love God above all else.

13: Ignite your desire to become righteous and virtuous.

14: Love others more than yourself. No excuses.

15: Remove distractions to hear clear communication from God.

16: Accept God's promises. They are designed for your well-being.

17: Replace the treasure in your heart with the treasure of God's Word.

18: Meditate on the words of God in the Bible every day.

19: Filter your thoughts. Put on the mind of Christ.

20: Redefine your life by asking yourself the right questions.

21: Pursue the right path. Fulfill biblical prophecy.

22: Rearrange your prayer requests to reflect heavenly mandates.

23: Use God's wisdom to make your decisions.

24: Be prepared to take radical risks if you want radical results.

25: The roots in your heart determine the fruits of your labor.

26: Turn your vineyard into a bountiful harvest for Christ's kingdom.

27: Focus your energy on completing kingdom activities.

28: Living a kingdom lifestyle is necessary to fulfill God's will.

29: The greatest return on investment is a human soul turning to Jesus.

30: Find and fulfill your responsibility to your Maker.

AUTHOR'S TESTIMONY

My hunt for the truth began in California. I grew up in the San Francisco Bay Area. It's one of the most spiritually diverse places on the planet. I was raised by a Protestant mother and a Catholic father. The Spanish heritage of my surname is Jewish. Most of my friends growing up, international or domestic, did not follow any particular religion.

I went through a spiritual identity crisis when I was younger. I could not stand the thought of being labeled. People who pushed their religion on me were met with sarcasm and ridicule. I have a deep appreciation for humanity at large and enjoy many cultures worldwide. I love people of all nationalities, appreciate unique languages, enjoy traveling far and wide, and embrace different ways of life. The thought of one religion, one way, or one truth seemed outrageous, simplistic, naïve, and too exclusive for me to want any part of. The thought of my friends of different beliefs or religions being sent to some place called hell was even more absurd; they were good people. Why would God do that?

I traveled the world extensively seeking the truth. After visiting more than fifty countries by age thirty, I felt I had a good handle on the world religions and could make an educated personal decision on faith. This was not based on my background or my family's beliefs but based on my own life experiences. One thing still stood in the way. I needed to read all the scriptures of the world religions cover to cover before I could make a final decision. I tend to research extensively before any major decision in my life, and this endeavor was certainly no exception to that rule. Thank goodness, because this exercise allowed me to uncover the real truth.

Admittedly, I had never read any of the scriptures of the world religions cover to cover until that point in my life. Once I did, the Bible shined like a diamond compared to the other world religions. The accurate prophecy, detailed history, and explanation of modern-day current events surprised me. The truth became evident. The Bible answered all of my skeptical questions. I frequently ask people who do not believe in Christ or the Bible's accuracy if they have ever read the Bible cover to cover. The answer is unanimously no.

On reflection, I now realize I'd been hearing the truth for a long time, even in my own home. I just wasn't listening. When I finally read the Bible cover to cover and absorbed the Word of God into my soul, it changed my life and my eternal destination. It will change yours as well.

ACKNOWLEDGEMENTS

Mission Finder was written for those who seek the truth, those who have found the truth, and for those who follow *the Way*. It's for those who desire to move from a place of salvation in their relationship with Jesus to a place of surrender in their relationship with Christ.

This book would not have come to fruition if it wasn't for the friendship and words of encouragement of Dr. David Jeremiah. Your leadership, inspiration, and motivation are second to none in my life. You are a true friend who inspires me and others through your preaching at Shadow Mountain Community Church and your worldwide ministry, Turning Point. Thank you for who you are in my life and your steadfast example of seeking Christ in everything you do.

To my beautiful wife, Megan, and my children, David and Emma, whose love and support have enabled me to focus on what is most important in life and prioritize our family vision, mission, and core values to reflect obedience to the Word of God.

To the entire Arroyo-Mazzola family for their prayers and support. To the leaders, agents, and staff members of AARE who have supported the vision of Mission Finder and Eye of a Needle Foundation from its inception.

To the Green family, founders of Hobby Lobby. To the Formsma family, founders of iLike Giving. Mart and Brad, your friendship and examples have led me to pursue a more generous lifestyle. Thank you for your guidance toward long-term kingdom investments that carry eternal value.

SPECIAL ACKNOWLEDGEMENT: MISSION FINDER'S HISTORY

A special thank you to Rod and Millie Gerhart, who developed the initial version of missionfinder.org in 1998 to help missionaries find mission trips online. You are an amazing couple, who together love the Lord so beautifully. May He richly bless your family for illustrating how to find and fulfill His will. Millions of visitors over the years have benefited from utilizing this service, and it has now been transformed to help users discover God's will for their lives through various Christian organizations in more than 170 countries.

I also owe my gratitude to David and Jan Malme, who have been instrumental in their stewardship of missionfinder.org, keeping the website operating smoothly and helping oversee the redevelopment throughout the seasons. Finally, a big thank you to all the staff members, interns, and volunteers who helped build and shape Eye of a Needle Foundation over the last decade to further God's kingdom. To Him be the glory.

That's the whole story. Here now is my final conclusion: Fear God and obey his commands, for this is everyone's duty. God will judge us for everything we do, including every secret thing, whether good or bad.
—Ecclesiastes 12:13-14 (NLT)

APPENDIX I

Day 3: God's Will

Throughout the Bible, God shares His will for your life.

+ God's will is for you to bring the kingdom of heaven to earth. (Matthew 6:10)
+ God's will is for you to bear fruit in your life. (John 15:8)
+ God's will is for you to make disciples. (Matthew 28:19)
+ God's will is for you to follow His will. (James 4:15)
+ God's will is that you seek His will in all that you do. (Proverbs 3:6)
+ God's will is to provide you a future and a hope. (Jeremiah 29:11)
+ God's will is that you find Him by praying to Him with all of your heart. (Jeremiah 29:12-13)
+ God's will is to give you the desires of your heart. (Psalm 37:4)
+ God's will is for you to be strong and courageous, not fearful. (Joshua 1:9)
+ God's will is for you to be grateful and thankful in all circumstances. (1 Thessalonians 5:18)
+ God's will is for you to renew your mind and not to conform to the ways of this world. (Romans 12:2)
+ God's will is for you to silence the ignorant talk of foolish people by your righteous behavior. (1 Peter 2:15)
+ God's will is for you to continue to do good in the midst of suffering. (1 Peter 4:19)
+ God's will is that you believe in Jesus and inherit eternal life. (John 3:16)
+ God's will is for you to find out if Jesus's teachings come from God. (John 7:17)
+ God's will is to love His followers like family. (Mark 3:35)
+ God's will is that you receive the reward He has promised. (Hebrews 10:36)

- God's will is to equip you with everything you need to carry out your mission. (Hebrews 13:21)
- God's will is to forgive you of all your sins and cleanse you from all unrighteousness. (1 John 1:9)
- God's will is for you to do what is right, to love mercy, and walk humbly with Him. (Micah 6:8)
- God's will is that you do all things through Him who strengthens you. (Philippians 4:13)
- God's will is that you acknowledge Him and trust Him with all of your heart and do not lean on your own understanding. (Proverbs 3:5)
- God's will is that you do not get caught up in worldly possessions or the desires of the eyes or the flesh. (1 John 2:16-17)
- God's will is to help strengthen you and to uphold you with righteousness. (Isaiah 41:10)
- God's will is for you to seek His presence continually and rely on His strength. (1 Chronicles 16:11)
- God's will is for you to love Him and be called according to His purpose. (Romans 8:28)
- God's will is to give to you generously and provide you wisdom. (James 1:5)
- God's will is for you to overcome temptation. (1 Corinthians 10:13)
- God's will is to supply every need of yours. (Philippians 4:19)
- God's will is that you live by the fruit of the Spirit. (Galatians 5:22-23)
- God's will is that you reject the acts of the flesh. (Galatians 5:19-21)
- God's will is that you should be sanctified. (1 Thessalonians 4:3)
- God's will is that you avoid sexual immorality. (1 Thessalonians 4:3)
- God's will is that you love Him above all else. (Luke 14:26)
- God's will is that no one should perish. (Matthew 18:12-14)
- God's will is that you seek the kingdom of God first in your life and everything will be added to you. (Matthew 6:33)
- God's will is that Jesus should lose none of the people who He gave to Jesus. (John 6:39)

Day 9: Follow Jesus

Here is a list of the things Jesus instructed us to do to help protect us from the ways of this world. The verses have been summarized.

+ Follow God's commandments. (John 14:21)
+ Store up treasures in heaven. (Matthew 6:20)
+ Keep watch and pray, so that you will not give in to temptation. (Matthew 26:41)
+ Forgive others and you will be forgiven. (Luke 6:37)
+ You must be born again. (John 3:5)
+ Teach new disciples to obey all of Jesus's commands. (Matthew 28:20)
+ You should tithe, but do not neglect the more important aspects of the law: justice, mercy, and faith. (Matthew 23:23)
+ Give, and you will receive. (Luke 6:38)
+ Give generously in private. God will notice it and reward you. (Matthew 6:4)
+ Use your possessions and finances to help others and make friends. This will benefit you in the long run. (Luke 16:9)
+ Do as Jesus has done to you. (John 13:15)
+ Do for the least of others as you would do for Jesus. (Matthew 25:40)
+ Before worshiping God, be reconciled with someone who has something against you. (Matthew 5:23-24)
+ Be happy and very glad when you are persecuted. (Matthew 5:11-12)
+ Be happy that Jesus is in heaven with the Father. (John 14:28)
+ Be ready at all times and keep watch for Jesus's return. (Matthew 24:42)
+ Learn to be shrewd as well as harmless. (Matthew 10:16)
+ Let your good deeds shine forth for all to see. (Matthew 5:16)
+ Let the spiritually dead bury their own dead. (Matthew 8:22)
+ Give to those in need, but do it very secretly. (Matthew 6:3)
+ Attempt to come to an agreement with your adversary even on the way to court. (Matthew 5:25)
+ When you fast, don't make it obvious—comb your hair and wash your face. (Matthew 6:16-17)

- When you get arrested, don't be anxious about what you will say. God's spirit will speak through you with the right words at the right time. (Matthew 10:19-20)
- When you see the hungry, feed them. When you see the thirsty, give them a drink. When you see a stranger, invite them into your home. When you see someone naked, give them clothing. When you see someone sick, care for them. When you see someone in prison, visit them. (Matthew 25:35-36)
- When you face difficulty or persecution in one city, run to another. (Matthew 10:23)
- When you obey God's commandments, you remain in His love. (John 15:10)
- Only fear God, who is able to send your body and soul to hell. (Matthew 10:28)
- Do not be scared of people who want to kill you. They can't hurt your soul by killing your body. (Matthew 10:28)
- Do not let anyone mislead you. Don't panic. (Matthew 24:4-6)
- Do not store up treasures here on earth. (Matthew 6:19)
- Don't make sacred promises. (Matthew 5:34)
- Do not say that you swear by heaven or by earth or by Jerusalem or by your head. (Matthew 5:34-36)
- Do not worry about everyday life. (Matthew 6:25)
- Do not worry about tomorrow. (Matthew 6:34)
- Don't be a judge of others. Then you won't be judged. (Luke 6:37)
- If you condemn other people, you will face that same condemnation. (Luke 6:37)
- Don't allow your heart to feel troubled. (John 14:1)
- Don't combat someone who is evil. (Matthew 5:39)
- Don't feel happy that spirits obey you, but be happy that your name is recorded in heaven. (Luke 10:20)
- Do not do kind acts in public to gain admiration. If you do, you will lose your heavenly reward. (Matthew 6:1)
- Don't sit in the seat of honor; sit at the foot of the table in the least seat. (Luke 14:8-10)
- To gain perfection, sell all you own to be generous to the needy and

gain heavenly treasure. Then follow Jesus. (Matthew 19:21)

+ Don't believe anyone who tries to tell you, "Here is the Messiah." (Mark 13:21)

+ If either hand makes you sin, remove it from your body and discard it. (Matthew 5:30)

+ If either eye creates lust in you, remove it from your body and discard it. (Matthew 5:29)

+ If you do what Jesus commands, you are His friend. (John 15:14)

+ God will judge you for being angry with someone. (Matthew 5:22)

+ You can be taken to court if you call others insulting names. (Matthew 5:22)

+ You may face hell if you curse other people. (Matthew 5:22)

+ Pretending even the smallest commandment doesn't exist and teaching other people to follow you in it will result in your demotion in the kingdom of God. (Matthew 5:19)

+ If you are obedient to God's commands and teach others to do the same, you will be promoted in God's kingdom. (Matthew 5:19)

+ Don't try to separate what God has put together. (Matthew 19:6)

+ Instead of vowing or swearing, just say yes or no and mean it. (Matthew 5:37)

+ Get rid of your own sin first, then you can help your friend deal with their sin. (Luke 6:42)

+ Repent and take on qualities of children to enter the kingdom of heaven. (Matthew 18:3)

+ Take communion to remember Jesus and to confirm God's covenant between God and His people. (Matthew 26:26-27)

+ Consume Jesus's words and commands through communion. (John 6:53-58)

+ God will hold us accountable if we refuse to forgive our brothers and sisters. (Matthew 18:23-35)

+ To be a true disciple, remain faithful to Jesus's commands. (John 8:31)

+ If you listen to Jesus's teachings and obey them, you are wise. (Matthew 7:24)

+ If you listen to Jesus's teachings and don't obey, you are a fool.

(Matthew 7:26)

+ Be obedient to religious leaders' teachings, but don't do what they do. They aren't obedient to their teachings. (Matthew 23:3)

Day 14: Discover God's Divine Design

Jesus reassures us of God's love in the Gospels through His teachings.

+ You are valuable to God. (Matthew 10:31)
+ God will care for you. (Luke 12:28)
+ God loves the world. He gave His one and only son. (John 3:16)
+ God loves you as much as He loves Jesus. (John 17:23)
+ God loved Jesus before the world began. (John 17:24)
+ God's love for Jesus is within Jesus's followers. (John 17:26)
+ God loves you dearly because you love Jesus and believe that He came from God. (John 16:27)
+ God's will is that all who see His son and believe in Him should have eternal life. (John 6:40)
+ Jesus desires you to be with Him. (John 17:24)
+ Jesus loves you like the Father loves Him. (John 15:9)
+ If you love Jesus, Father God will love you. (John 14:21)
+ Jesus will reveal Himself to those who love Him. (John 14:21)
+ Anyone who believes in Jesus will not perish but have eternal life. (John 3:16)
+ Jesus came to serve, not to be served. (Matthew 20:28)
+ Jesus came to give His life as a ransom for many. (Matthew 20:28)
+ Jesus gave Himself as a holy sacrifice for you so you can be made holy by God's truth. (John 17:19)
+ The greatest love is to lay down your life for your friends. (John 15:13)
+ Our love for each other will prove to the world we are Jesus's disciples. (John 13:35)

Day 16: Accept God's Promises

Start today by taking the time to meditate on a handful of His promises. Discover more on your own by opening God's treasure chest of promises, the Bible.

+ The world doesn't know God, but Jesus does. (John 17:25)
+ God and Jesus are one. (John 17:21)
+ God's Word is the truth. (John 17:17)
+ We are united with God through the name of Jesus. (John 17:11)
+ Jesus gave us God's Word. (John 17:14)
+ The names of God and Jesus are powerful and protect us. (John 17:11-12)
+ Everything Jesus has is a gift from God. (John 17:7)
+ God gave Jesus authority over everyone. (John 17:2)
+ God knows exactly what you need even before you ask. (Matthew 6:8)
+ God gives sunshine and rain to good people and bad people. (Matthew 5:45)
+ Jesus's words won't ever disappear, even after heaven and earth are gone. (Matthew 24:35)
+ Jesus is the source of David and heir to his throne. (Revelation 22:16)
+ Jesus is the bright morning star. (Revelation 22:16)
+ Jesus is the Alpha and Omega, the First and Last, the Beginning and the End. (Revelation 22:13)
+ God is more powerful than anyone else. (John 10:29)
+ The Father is greater than His son, Jesus. (John 14:28)
+ There will be multiple false prophets, and many people will believe their deceptions. (Matthew 24:11)
+ Many people will stop following Jesus and choose betrayal and hatred. (Matthew 24:10)
+ If you endure all the way to the end, you will be saved. (Matthew 24:13)
+ Jesus will raise up His followers on the last day. (John 6:40, 54)

- It is foolish to be rich in earthly things but not in your relationship with God. (Luke 12:21)
- It will be difficult for a rich person to enter God's kingdom. It would be easier to get a camel through the eye of a needle. (Matthew 19:23-24)
- You need to be more righteous than the teachers of the law and Pharisees to enter the kingdom of heaven. (Matthew 5:20)
- You get eternal life by knowing the one true God and Jesus, whom He sent. (John 17:3)
- Jesus is the bread of life that came down from heaven. Anyone who eats the bread of heaven will live forever and never die. (John 6:47-51)
- Believers have moved from death to life, so they will not be condemned for sinning. (John 5:24)
- The Father sent His son to earth to save it, not to judge it. (John 3:17)
- The angels of God rejoice when one sinner repents. (Luke 15:10)
- Anything is possible with God. (Matthew 19:26)

Day 20: Redefine Your Life

Jesus asked questions on obedience, discernment, and intentions. All are quoted from the NIV.

Jesus questions your obedience to reveal your loyalty.

- *"Why do you call me, 'Lord, Lord,' and do not do what I say?"* (Luke 6:46)
- *"How will you escape being condemned to hell?"* (Matthew 23:33)
- *"Do you understand what I have done for you?"* (John 13:12)
- *"However, when the Son of Man comes, will he find faith on the earth?"* (Luke 18:8)

Jesus questions your discernment to open your eyes.

- *"Why is my language not clear to you?"* (John 8:43)
- *"Why do you look at the speck of sawdust in your brother's eye and pay no attention to the plank in your own eye?"* (Matthew 7:3)

- "How can you believe since you accept glory from one another but do not seek the glory that comes from the only God?" (John 5:44)
- "And will not God bring about justice for his chosen ones, who cry out to him day and night? Will he keep putting them off?" (Luke 18:7)
- "For who is greater, the one who is at the table or the one who serves?" (Luke 22:27)
- "So if you have not been trustworthy in handling worldly wealth, who will trust you with true riches?" (Luke 16:11)
- "Did not the one who made the outside make the inside also?" (Luke 11:40)
- "Salt is good, but if it loses its saltiness, how can you make it salty again?" (Mark 9:50)
- "Why then is it written that the Son of Man must suffer much and be rejected?" (Mark 9:12)
- "Why are you talking about having no bread? Do you still not see or understand? Are your hearts hardened? Do you have eyes but fail to see, and ears but fail to hear? And don't you remember?" (Mark 8:17-18)
- "Do you still not understand?" (Mark 8:21)
- "But how then would the Scriptures be fulfilled that say it must happen in this way?" (Matthew 26:54)
- "Have you never read in the Scriptures …?" (Matthew 21:42)
- "What do you think about the Messiah? Whose son is he?" (Matthew 22:42)
- "Which is greater: the gold, or the temple that makes the gold sacred? … Which is greater: the gift, or the altar that makes the gift sacred?" (Matthew 23:17, 19)
- "Who do people say the Son of Man is?" (Matthew 16:13)
- "Who do you say I am?" (Matthew 16:15)
- "Why do you ask me about what is good?" (Matthew 19:17)

Jesus questions your intentions to uncover your motives.

- "Why are you thinking these things?" (Mark 2:8)
- "Does this offend you?" (John 6:61)
- "What is it you want?" (Matthew 20:21)

- *"What good will it be for someone to gain the whole world, yet forfeit their soul? Or what can anyone give in exchange for their soul?"* (Matthew 16:26)
- *"Why do you break the command of God for the sake of your tradition?"* (Matthew 15:3)
- *"If you love those who love you, what reward will you get?"* (Matthew 5:46)
- *"If you greet only your own people, what are you doing more than others?"* (Matthew 5:47)
- *"Why are you trying to trap me?"* (Matthew 22:18)
- *"Why do you call me good?"* (Mark 10:18)
- *"What do you want me to do for you?"* (Mark 10:51)
- *"Why are you thinking these things in your hearts?"* (Luke 5:22)
- *"Why are you trying to kill me?"* (John 7:19)
- *"Why are you angry with me for healing a man's whole body on the Sabbath?"* (John 7:23)
- *"Can any of you prove me guilty of sin?"* (John 8:46)
- *"Why then do you accuse me of blasphemy because I said, 'I am God's Son'?"* (John 10:36)
- *"Who is it you want?"* (John 18:4, 7)
- *"Why question me?"* (John 18:21)
- *"If I spoke the truth, why did you strike me?"* (John 18:23)
- *"Do you love me?"* (John 21:17)

Day 23: Calibrate Your Decisions with Wisdom

Throughout the Gospels, Jesus illustrates cause and effect. He shows you with heavenly insight how your choices and decisions directly impact your life and eternal well-being.

- *"You must give an account on judgment day for every idle word you speak."* (Matthew 12:36 NLT)
- *"The words you say will either acquit you or condemn you."* (Matthew 12:37 NLT)

+ *"Your faith has made you well."* (Matthew 9:22 NLT)
+ *"Anything is possible if a person believes."* (Mark 9:23 NLT)
+ *"Your faith has saved you; go in peace."* (Luke 7:50 NLT)
+ *"Everyone who acknowledges me [Jesus] publicly here on Earth, I will also acknowledge before my Father in heaven."* (Matthew 10:32 NLT)
+ *"But everyone who denies me [Jesus] here on Earth, I will also deny before my Father in heaven."* (Matthew 10:33 NLT)
+ *"For if you forgive other people when they sin against you, your heavenly Father will also forgive you."* (Matthew 6:14 NIV)
+ *"But if you do not forgive others their sins, your Father will not forgive your sins."* (Matthew 6:15 NIV)
+ *"Whoever feeds on this bread [Jesus] will live forever."* (John 6:58 NIV)
+ *"Believe in the light [Jesus] while you have the light, so that you may become children of the light."* (John 12:36 NIV)
+ *"Anyone who believes and is baptized will be saved."* (Mark 16:16 NLT)
+ *"Anyone who refuses to believe will be condemned."* (Mark 16:16 NLT)
+ *"Anyone who believes in me [Jesus] will do the same works I have done, and even greater works."* (John 14:12 NLT)
+ *"Those who exalt themselves will be humbled, and those who humble themselves will be exalted."* (Matthew 23:12 NIV)
+ *"When you pray, do not be like the hypocrites, for they love to pray standing in the synagogues and on the street corners to be seen by others."* (Matthew 6:5 NIV)
+ *"When you pray, go into your room, close the door and pray to your Father, who is unseen. Then your Father, who sees what is done in secret, will reward you."* (Matthew 6:6 NIV)

APPENDIX 2

Scripture quotes are labeled with the translation they are taken from.
Other entries are references to Scripture or outside sources.

Day 1

1. Matthew 7:14 (NLT)
2. Matthew 7:21-23 (NLT, emphasis added)
3. Ephesians 2:8-9 (NIV)
4. Luke 7:50 (NKJV)
5. Matthew 7:21 (NLT, emphasis added)
6. Matthew 7:23 (NLT, emphasis added)
7. Matthew 7:24 (NLT)
8. Matthew 7:26 (NLT)
9. John 14:23 (NIV)
10. Matthew 5:18 (NLT)
11. Proverbs 7:2 (NIV)
12. Psalm 37:28 (NKJV)
13. Jeremiah 32:19 (NIV)
14. Psalm 40:8 (NIV)
15. 1 Peter 2:9 (NKJV)
16. Ephesians 2:10 (NKJV)
17. Luke 6:46 (NIV)

Day 2

1. John 6:40 (NIV)
2. Luke 4:18 (NIV)
3. John 6:38
4. John 14:31
5. John 15:10
6. John 15:10
7. John 14:31
8. John 5:19
9. Matthew 26:39
10. John 10:30
11. Matthew 6:33
12. John 15:13, John 10:15
13. Luke 4:18
14. John 12:50
15. John 18:28-40
16. Matthew 6:33
17. Mark 4:26-27
18. Psalm 23:1 (NIV)
19. Proverbs 1:7 (NKJV)
20. Matthew 18:3 (NIV)
21. Psalm 25:15 (NIV)
22. Psalm 25:14 (NIV)
23. Proverbs 9:10 (NIV)
24. John 18:11 (NIV)

Day 3

1. Proverbs 3:5-6 (NLT)
2. Proverbs 1:23 (NLT)
3. Joshua 1:9
4. Isaiah 41:10
5. Proverbs 3:5
6. 1 John 2:16-17
7. 1 Thessalonians 5:18
8. 1 Thessalonians 4:3
9. 1 Thessalonians 4:3
10. 1 Peter 2:15
11. Romans 12:2
12. Galatians 5:22-23
13. Romans 8:28

14. James 4:15
15. Jeremiah 29:11
16. James 1:5
17. Luke 14:26
18. Psalm 37:4
19. 1 John 1:9
20. 1 Corinthians 10:13
21. John 3:16
22. Matthew 28:19
23. Mark 3:35
24. John 15:8
25. Matthew 6:10
26. Hebrews 10:36
27. Matthew 6:33
28. Hebrews 13:21
29. 1 Chronicles 16:11
30. Philippians 4:19
31. Proverbs 3:6
32. Jeremiah 29:12-13
33. 1 Peter 4:19
34. John 7:17
35. Micah 6:8
36. Philippians 4:13
37. Galatians 5:19-21
38. Matthew 18:12-14
39. John 6:39
40. John 6:70 (NIV)

Day 4

1. Luke 2:49 (NKJV)
2. Luke 2:49 (NKJV)
3. Matthew 25:31-34 (NIV)
4. Matthew 25:14-29 (NLT, emphasis added)
5. Jeremiah 31:33-34 (NKJV)
6. Matthew 13:47-49 (NLT)

7. Matthew 13:24-26, 28-30 (NIV)
8. Luke 16:3-6, 8-12 (NIV)
9. Proverbs 23:5 (NIV)
10. John 14:15-17, 19-20 (NIV)
11. Psalm 31:23 (NIV)
12. Luke 2:49 (NKJV)

Mission Finder Story:
One Flight From Heaven's Door
1. "Police: Plot to blow up aircraft foiled." August 10, 2006. CNN, www.cnn.com/2006/WORLD/europe/08/10/uk.terror

Day 5

1. Proverbs 29:18 (KJV)
2. Matthew 6:9-10 (NKJV)
3. John 14:28
4. John 14:2
5. Matthew 24:44
6. John 14:18
7. John 14:3
8. Luke 12:37
9. Matthew 24:40-41
10. John 14:2
11. John 20:29
12. John 14:19
13. Psalm 27:1 (NIV)
14. Matthew 5:16 (NKJV)
15. Luke 24:38 (NIV)

Day 6

1. Matthew 6:33 (NLT)
2. Ephesians 4:11-12 (NKJV)
3. Psalm 37:3 (NIV, emphasis added)

4. Psalm 37:7 (NIV)
5. Matthew 6:6 (NIV)
6. Habakkuk 2:2-3 (NIV)
7. Isaiah 64:8 (NIV)
8. John 6:38-40 (NIV)
9. Matthew 20:32 (NIV)

Day 7
1. John 16:33 (NLT)
2. Matthew 6:24 (NIV)
3. Matthew 6:25 (NLT)
4. John 15:11 (NIV)
5. Psalm 1:1 (NLT)
6. Philemon 1:7 (NLT)
7. John 15:9-11 (NLT)
8. John 15:14 (NLT, emphasis added)
9. Psalm 5:12 (NIV)
10. Matthew 5:11-12 (NLT)
11. Luke 6:38 (NLT)
12. David Green (founder of Hobby Lobby), in discussion with the author, May 25, 2016, in Hobby Lobby Headquarters, Oklahoma City, OK.
13. Solomon, Brian. "David Green: The Biblical Billionaire Backing The Evangelical Movement." Forbes. (October 8, 2012.) www.forbes.com/sites/ briansolomon/2012/09/18/ david-green-the-biblical- billionaire-backing-the- evangelical-movement.
14. Matthew 23:23 (NLT)
15. Matthew 5:6 (NLT)

16. John 15:14 (NLT)
17. Matthew 7:23
18. Psalm 1:6 (NLT)
19. James 1:2-3 (NIV)
20. John 5:6 (NIV)

Day 8
1. John 16:33 (NLT)
2. Luke 22:42 (NIV)
3. Matthew 7:21 (NIV)
4. Psalm 6:3 (NLT)
5. Psalm 6:2 (NKJV)
6. Psalm 6:4 (NIV)
7. Psalm 6:9 (NIV)
8. Psalm 6:8 (NIV)
9. Proverbs 27:17 (NIV)
10. Galatians 5:22-23 (NKJV)
11. Matthew 22:42 (NKJV)

Mission Finder Story:
Loving One By One
1. Rice, Xan. "Uganda bomb blast kills at least 74." July 12, 2010. *The Guardian*. www.theguardian. com/world/2010/jul/12/uganda- kampala-bombs-explosions- attacks
2. Matthew 5:7 (NLT)

Day 9
1. Matthew 10:38 (NIV)
2. John 17:6 (NLT)
3. John 14:21
4. Matthew 6:20
5. Matthew 26:41
6. Matthew 7:24

7. John 8:31
8. Matthew 5:16
9. Luke 6:38
10. John 13:15
11. Luke 6:37
12. John 3:5
13. Matthew 28:20
14. Proverbs 2:20 (NIV)
15. Psalm 118:8 (NKJV)
16. Matthew 7:13-14 (NIV)
17. John 13:12 (NIV)

Day 10
1. Mark 9:23 (NLT)
2. Matthew 19:26 (NKJV)
3. Romans 8:31 (NKJV)
4. Deuteronomy 31:6 (NKJV)
5. Matthew 11:28-30 (NKJV)
6. Psalm 4:1 (NIV)
7. Mark 4:40 (NIV)

Day 11
1. Psalm 127:1 (NKJV)
2. Matthew 10:39 (NLT)
3. Psalm 33:18 (NIV)
4. Psalm 4:8 (NKJV)
5. Matthew 6:21 (NLT)
6. Matthew 6:27 (NIV)

Day 12
1. Matthew 28:19 (NIV, emphasis added)
2. Matthew 10:37 (NIV)
3. Matthew 13:3-8 (NIV, emphasis added)
4. Matthew 13:18-23 (NIV, emphasis added)
5. 1 John 2:17 (NIV, emphasis added)
6. Matthew 16:26 (NIV)
7. Psalm 37:5-6 (NKJV)
8. Psalm 25:12-13 (NIV)
9. Revelation 4:11 (NIV)
10. Matthew 16:26 (NIV)

Part II
Introduction
1. Ephesians 1:9 (NLT)
2. Matthew 22:37-39 (NIV)
3. John 15:9-10 (NKJV)
4. John 8:31-32 (NLT)
5. Matthew 28:20 (NLT)
6. John 15:12 (NIV)
7. John 13:35 (NIV)

Day 13
1. Psalm 11:7 (NIV)
2. Psalm 11:5 (NIV)
3. Micah 6:8 (NIV)
4. John 14:21 (NKJV)
5. Psalm 18:28 (NIV)
6. Psalm 119:105 (NIV)
7. John 1:5 (NIV)
8. Luke 11:36 (NLT)
9. John 8:12 (NIV)
10. Matthew 5:16 (NIV)
11. John 18:4 (NIV)

Day 14
1. Luke 6:31 (NLT)
2. Matthew 10:31
3. Luke 12:28

4. John 6:40
5. John 17:24
6. John 15:9
7. John 14:21
8. John 3:16
9. Matthew 20:28
10. Matthew 20:28
11. John 17:19
12. John 15:13
13. John 13:35
14. Luke 6
15. John 13:34
16. Matthew 5:44
17. Luke 6:30
18. Luke 6:28
19. Luke 6:27
20. Luke 6:28
21. Luke 6:32
22. Luke 6:29
23. Luke 6:29
24. Luke 6:34
25. Luke 10:33-37
26. Matthew 22:39 (NLT)
27. David P. Jeremiah, *A Life Beyond Amazing*, (Tennessee, W Publishing Group, Thomas Nelson, 2017)
28. Galatians 5:22-23 (NIV)
29. Matthew 5:46 (NIV)

Day 15
1. 1 Timothy 4:16 (NLT)
2. Psalm 23:1-3 (NIV)
3. Proverbs 3:24 (NKJV)
4. John 5:24 (NLT, emphasis added)

5. Romans 10:17 (NKJV)
6. Matthew 5:4 (NIV)
7. John 8:43 (NIV)

Day 16
1. Psalm 12:6 (NKJV)
2. Hebrews 13:8 (NKJV)
3. Proverbs 7:1 (NKJV)
4. John 17:11
5. John 17:11-12
6. John 3:17
7. John 17:3
8. John 17:17
9. Matthew 19:26
10. John 6:47-51
11. Matthew 6:8
12. Psalm 40:8 (NLT)
13. John 10:29
14. John 17:21
15. John 17:2
16. Revelation 22:13
17. Matthew 24:35
18. Matthew 24:11
19. John 6:40, 54
20. Luke 12:21
21. Matthew 5:20
22. John 8:46 (NIV)

Mission Finder Story:
Through The Eye Of A Needle
1. Matthew 19:23-24 (NKJV)
2. Matthew 19:25-26 (NKJV)

Day 17
1. Matthew 4:4 (NKJV)
2. Luke 11:34-35 (NIV)

3. Matthew 12:35 (NLT)
4. Mark 7:21-22 (NLT)
5. Matthew 12:34 (NLT)
6. Matthew 12:33 (NLT)
7. "AMA offers 6 tips to improve heart health during American Heart Month." January 30, 2020. American Medical Association. www.ama-assn.org/press-center/press-releases/ama-offers-6-tips-improve-heart-health-during-american-heart-month
8. 1 Peter 5:7 (NLT)
9. Ezekiel 36:26 (NIV)
10. Matthew 9:4 (NIV)

Day 18
1. Hebrews 4:12 (NKJV)
2. Ephesians 6:17 (NIV)
3. Psalm 119:72 (NIV)
4. Psalm 78:4 (NLT)
5. Proverbs 3:19 (NIV)
6. Proverbs 2:3 (NLT)
7. Proverbs 2:10 (NLT)
8. Hebrews 4:12
9. Psalm 1:2 (NIV)
10. Proverbs 16:31 (NKJV)
11. Matthew 21:42 (NKJV)

Day 19
1. Mark 7:20 (NLT)
2. 1 Peter 3:17 (NKJV)
3. Psalm 7:14 (NLT)
4. Mark 1:35 (NIV)
5. Psalm 7:1 (NLT)
6. Psalm 7:10 (NIV)

7. John 6:70 (NIV)
8. Luke 24:26 (NIV)
9. Luke 10:26 (NIV)
10. Mark 4:21 (NIV)
11. Mark 10:3 (NIV)
12. Matthew 6:27 (NIV)
13. Matthew 6:28 (NIV)
14. Mark 4:40 (NIV)
15. John 8:46 (NIV)
16. John 5:47 (NKJV)
17. John 3:12 (NIV)
18. Luke 24:38 (NIV)
19. Luke 8:25 (NIV)
20. Matthew 9:28 (NIV)
21. Matthew 9:4 (NIV)
22. Matthew 14:31 (NIV)
23. Psalm 139:1-4 (NIV)
24. 1 Corinthians 2:16
25. Mark 2:8 (NIV)

Day 20
1. Luke 12:31 (NLT)
2. Proverbs 3:19 (NKJV)
3. John 10:10
4. Luke 6:46 (NIV)
5. Matthew 23:33 (NIV)
6. John 13:12 (NIV)
7. Matthew 7:3 (NIV)
8. Luke 22:27 (NIV)
9. Luke 11:40 (NIV)
10. Matthew 16:26 (NIV)
11. Matthew 5:46 (NIV)
12. Luke 5:22 (NIV)
13. Mark 8:21 (NIV)

Day 21

1. 1 Chronicles 16:11 (NIV)
2. Matthew 6:19-20 (NKJV)
3. Acts 1:8 (NLT)
4. Psalm 1:3 (NIV)
5. Malachi 3:10 (NIV)
6. Matthew 6:3-4 (NIV)
7. Matthew 6:5 (NIV)
8. Matthew 24:14 (NKJV)
9. Matthew 28:18-20
10. Mart Green and Todd Peterson, in discussion with the author. For more information on illumiNations, see https://illuminations.bible/.
11. "How many languages are there in the world?" Ethnologue. Accessed Sept. 1, 2020. www.ethnologue.com/guides/how-many-languages
12. Psalm 1:2 (NIV)
13. Proverbs 1:2 (NLT)
14. Proverbs 1:5 (NLT)
15. John 1:38 (NIV)

Day 22

1. Psalm 5:2-3 (NIV)
2. 2 Chronicles 1:10-12 (NIV)
3. Galatians 5:17 (NIV)
4. Acts 5:32 (NIV)
5. 2 Thessalonians 1:11-12 (NKJV)
6. Matthew 6:9-13 (NLT, numbers added)
7. Matthew 6:8 (NIV)
8. Matthew 6:6
9. John 16:26

10. Mark 11:25
11. John 16:23
12. Mark 11:24, Matthew 21:22
13. John 14:14
14. Matthew 7:8
15. Matthew 7:11
16. John 17:1
17. John 17:5
18. John 17:15
19. John 17:17
20. John 17:17
21. Matthew 6:7 (NIV)
22. Matthew 18:19 (NKJV)
23. Mark 10:51 (NIV)

Day 23

1. Proverbs 3:5 (NKJV)
2. Psalm 37:3 (NKJV)
3. Proverbs 8:17 (NKJV)
4. Proverbs 8:35 (NIV)
5. Proverbs 1:7 (NLT)
6. Proverbs 2:11 (NLT)
7. Matthew 12:37 (NLT)
8. Matthew 9:22 (NLT)
9. Mark 9:23 (NLT)
10. Matthew 10:32 (NLT)
11. Matthew 6:14 (NIV)
12. John 6:58 (NIV)
13. John 14:12 (NLT)
14. Matthew 23:12 (NIV)
15. Matthew 23:33 (NIV)

Day 24

1. Matthew 19:29 (NIV)
2. Proverbs 2:20 (NKJV)
3. Proverbs 2:6 (NKJV)

4.   Proverbs 3:19 (NKJV)

5.   Luke 8:25 (NIV)

Mission Finder Story:
Choosing To Be Present

1.   Isaiah 6:8 (NIV)

2.   Psalm 46:10

Day 25

1.   Matthew 7:16 (NKJV)

2.   Matthew 7:17-20 (NLT)

3.   Psalm 9:1 (NLT)

4.   Psalm 5:7 (NLT)

5.   Psalm 5:11 (NIV)

6.   Luke 11:40 (NIV)

Day 26

1.   Luke 8:15 (NLT)

2.   Psalm 1:3 (NIV)

3.   John 4:14 (NIV)

4.   Matthew 5:13 (NIV)

5.   John 15:2 (NLT)

6.   Matthew 9:37 (NLT)

7.   Psalm 90:17 (NIV)

8.   Psalm 26:12 (NLT)

9.   John 15:20 (NLT)

10.   1 Peter 4:12-13 (NLT)

11.   Matthew 27:12-14 (NKJV)

12.   Luke 22:42 (NLT)

13.   Psalm 27:14 (NLT)

14.   Matthew 9:28 (NIV)

Day 27

1.   John 4:34 (NLT)

2.   Matthew 25:35-36 (NIV, numbers added)

3.   Matthew 25:40 (NIV)

4.   Matthew 25:42 (NIV)

5.   Proverbs 5:2 (NLT)

6.   Psalm 30:5 (NKJV)

7.   Psalm 31:14 (NKJV)

8.   Mark 4:30 (NIV)

Day 28

1.   1 Samuel 15:22 (NLT)

2.   Proverbs 2:8 (NKJV)

3.   Psalm 31:23 (NLT)

4.   Matthew 5:6 (NKJV)

5.   2 Corinthians 3:18 (NKJV)

6.   John 16:13 (NLT)

7.   John 16:13 (NLT)

8.   John 14:26 (NLT)

9.   John 14:26 (NLT)

10.   John 3:6 (NLT)

11.   John 14:17 (NLT)

12.   John 16:13 (NKJV)

13.   John 16:8 (NLT)

14.   John 16:15 (NLT)

15.   John 4:24 (NLT)

16.   John 3:5 (NLT)

17.   Proverbs 7:3 (NLT)

18.   2 Timothy 4:2 (NIV)

19.   Mark 4:21 (NIV)

Day 29

1.   Mark 1:17 (NLT)

2.   John 14:26 (NIV)

3.   Matthew 11:15 (NIV)

4.   Psalm 40:10 (NIV)

5.   Matthew 13:9 (NIV)

6.   John 15:20 (NLT)

7.   Psalm 9:11 (NLT)

8. Luke 12:8 (NLT)
9. Mark 16:15 (NLT)
10. Matthew 10:7 (NIV)
11. Matthew 28:19 (NLT)
12. Matthew 12:31-32 (NIV)
13. Psalm 9:8-9 (NLT)
14. John 21:5 (NIV)

Day 30
1. Matthew 7:21-23 (NLT, emphasis added)
2. John 17:1-5
3. Matthew 22:37
4. John 4:24
5. Luke 12:31
6. John 14:1
7. John 15:9
8. Luke 14:26
9. Matthew 10:38 (NLT)
10. Matthew 10:37 (NLT)
11. Matthew 6:24 (NLT)
12. Luke 18:8 (NIV)

CONTACT INFORMATION

www.AndrewArroyo.com

Made in the USA
Columbia, SC
05 September 2021